THE RIGHT OF CONQUEST MADNESS IN MATABELELAND

THE RIGHT OF CONQUEST MADNESS IN MATABELELAND

JONATHAN MAPHENDUKA

Copyright @ 2020 by Jonathan Maphenduka

ISBN: Hardcover   978 1 7334237 2 4
        Softcover   978 1 7334237 1 7
        eBook   978 1 7334237 0 0

Published by Kiye Media

Kiye Media Inc., 4160 Logan Dr. #1969, Loganville, GA 30052 USA

All rights reserved. No part of this book may be reproduced, scanned, or distributed in any printed or electronic form without permission. Please do not participate in or encourage piracy of copyrighted materials in violation of the author's rights. Purchase only authorised editions.

For information about permission to reproduce selections from this book, write to permissions@kiyemedia.com or to Permissions 4160 Logan Drive # 1969, Loganville, GA 30052 USA

To Order additional copies of this book, contact:
Kiye Media
www.kiyemedia.com
orders@kiyemedia.com

Contents

Contents vii
Foreword ix

CHAPTER 1
FROM MARICO VALLEY TO MATABELELAND 1
CHAPTER 2
BOERS OUTRACED BY THE BRITISH 24
CHAPTER 3
A POINT OF NO RETURN 28
CHAPTER 4
THE VICTORIA INCIDENT 59
CHAPTER 5
THE FATAL DAY 74
CHAPTER 6
THE SECRET AGREEMENT 77
CHAPTER 7
AFTERMATH OF THE SECRET AGREEMENT 89
CHAPTER 8
WEAPONRY OF PRECISION AGAINST ASSEGAIS 93
CHAPTER 9
SOUTH AFRICAN NATIONAL CONGRESS PETITION 106
CIIAPTER 10
ORDERS IN COUNCIL AND THEIR MEANING 112

CHAPTER 11
ORDERS-IN-COUNCIL REGULARIZED 119
CHAPTER 12
PASSING THE BUCK 124
CHAPTER 13
NYAMANDE THE ENIGMA 143
CHAPTER 14
NYAMANDE'S SOUTH AFRICAN CONTACTS 152
CHAPTER 15
NYAMANDE'S EPIC LETTERS 168
CHAPTER 16
SUPERINTEDENT OF NATIVES'S VIEW 175
CHAPTER 17
PRINCE ARTHUR'S REBUFF 179
CHAPTER 18
NYAMANDE THE KING 185
CHAPTER 19
RHODES THE DESPOT 190
CHAPTER 20
THE NJUBE DEBACLE 203
CHAPTER 21
MUGABE DISOWNS GWEBU PEOPLE 212
CHAPTER 22
THE RIGHT OF CONQUEST INSANITY 221

ABOUT AUTHOR .... A
ABREVIATIONS AND ACRONYMS C
BIBLIOGRAPHY .... E

THE RIGHT OF CONQUEST MADNESS IN MATABELELAND

Foreword

ENOUGH has been written about Mzilikazi's leaving Zululand to settle in what became Matabeleland. Very little, however, has been said about British policy of extermination, the war of attrition and scorched-earth-policy the invaders applied to smash the greatest kingdom south of the Sahara. Lobengula's warriors in that lightning and tragic campaign which began early in October 1893, lost 6 000 men in one battlefield alone against less than 500 British troops (all told) who too died during the entire war and the uprising that followed in 1896. There was a notable loss of 34 British troops in one encounter during the Battle of Lower Shangani when the men led by Alan Wilson fought gallantly against numerically superior Matabele impis, where the Warriors lost 900 men. These are the men who are buried at Pupu in the Lupane forests. But even this single feat by the Warriors provides little solace when devastating weapons of precision were used against the Warriors who bore primitive assegais and battle axes.

Moreover, little has been written about Lobengula's numerous efforts to avert a war with the British that he was sure he could not win by any means. Lobengula's peace overtures and efforts were not only frustrated by Cecil John Rhodes and his hatchet man, Leander Starr Jameson, but the activities of enemy forces often led to tragedy as manifested by the murder of two of the king's envoys with a peace letter to be delivered to Queen Victoria's representative in Palapye in Bechuanaland.

When faced, not only with forces of the Chartered Company in the west and the east, but also with the Boers in the south bank of the Limpopo River, Lobengula often quoted King Mzilikazi's treaties with the Transvaal which began in 1853, culminating in the Grobler Treaty of 1887. Both those treaties should have led the Matabele Kingdom into the South African Republic's sphere of influence. Lobengula's peace efforts, however, were not only spurned or ignored by the Republic but were also actively frustrated by the Chartered Company led on the ground by that impulsive and sabre-rattling libertine, Leander Starr Jameson, whose only concern was the defeat of Lobengula at any cost to "teach the Matabele a lesson of their life". The Anglo-Matabele war ushered fame, instead of infamy, to the invaders, a fame whose glory was echoed with so much relish across the globe following Lobengula's disappearance.

However, the Matabele Warriors, essentially armed with primitive weapons, did give a fair account of themselves against heavy odds, and this led to British xenophobia against them which is manifested to this day. The Matabele Kingdom became the only one in Southern Africa to be denied British protection despite the fact that the Kingdom went begging for it and Britain had signed two treaties of friendship with Mzilikazi and Lobengula. This book is a historical and political satire that seeks to highlight some of the war crimes which were committed by the invading British forces using devastating precision and heavy weaponry. The devastating Maxim gun and artillery was used in the Anglo-Matabele for the first time in Africa to "smash and teach the Matabele a lesson of their life'.'

The book *The Right of Conquest Madness in Matabeleland*

seeks to unveil some of the unknown tragic events that led to that war with Rhodes' armed forces, a war that was precipitated by criminal intrigue and conspiracy on the part of the Chartered Company which forced it on Lobengula.

Not even Lobengula's two bags of gold sovereigns sent to Patrick Forbes as a propitiation for peace was enough to purchase that peace once the war began. And yet Lobengula is often held out by modern writers and historians as a blood-thirsty villain. His detractors often overlook the inevitability of war that he could not stop by any means even if he wanted to.

It is often ignored that Lobengula faced an array of forces and formidable odds as the enemy mounted pressure resulting from the scramble for his country in which, unlike his father Mzilikazi before him, Lobengula found himself faced with. And thanks to the array of armour which that despotic Cecil John Rhodes had assembled, the war, as feared, was launched leading to excesses that came close to extermination of the Matabele.

With the stage now reached for the publication of this book, it is now time for me to thank Canaan Munjeri and those others who provided some information used in this book. Of particular importance was his information pertaining to the plight of the Khoi Sans who were taken from South Africa to Europe during the right of conquest period which was applied by colonists. The barbaric manner in which the victims of the right of conquest were treated led to the institution of the Nuremberg Principles after World War II.

This book is dedicated to Mzilikazi kaMatshobana the founder of the great nation of Mthwakazi whose leadership in nation-building has no parallel in Africa.

CHAPTER 1

FROM MARICO VALLEY TO MATABELELAND

WHEN Mzilikazi left Zululand following his refusal to surrender the booty of war to Tshaka his mentor, for 10 years he settled in Marico Valley in the Northern Cape. However, some 30 years later saw him settled across the Limpopo River in what became his Matabele Kingdom. This was in 1838 and the kingdom flourished, until British colonists invaded it and set in motion a process of destruction that finally brought an end of the most formidable kingdom in Africa.

It took the use of precision weapons of war that left a trail of blood and immolation as the British applied a policy of extermination and attrition "to teach the Matabele a lesson of life". But it took five years of preparation for the invading forces to launch a devastating onslaught in which the lives of civilians were not spared. This callous enterprise of dishonour, injustice and bloody-mindedness was pursued to its logical conclusion in the name of what the colonists called white civilization.

When, one might ask, does white civilization become bedfellows with barbarism? History must record that this became a fact when British South Africa Company mercenaries in 1893 invaded the Kingdom of Mthwakazi that in 1894 became Matabeleland.

From Marico Valley he was driven away by Dutch trekkers led by Maritz and Potgieter. Apart from war, there was nothing that might have tempted or forced Mzilikazi to cross the Limpopo into the plateau between the

Limpopo and the Zambezi. The Marico Valley had all that satisfied any heart's desire. The Marico Valley is a marvel of cattle and agricultural land, probably without equal in South Africa. The valley is a great expanse of land where the Boers used lethal arms of war to keep everyone out, including the British.

During a recent travel through the northern tip of the valley, I saw written on a farm gate the jarring words "Kom Kaffir", a warning, I believe, that told trespassers to keep their distance from the farm. It also told me how – depending on how one viewed it - democracy is working or being abused in South Africa. It is probably only in post-apartheid South Africa where black South Africans can still openly be called Kaffirs! That warning had another message: the attachment to the land that anyone occupying it may experience.

The Marico Valley has been home for Afrikaners since the advent of Maritz and Potgieter in the early 1830s, when the Great Trek north led the trekkers to the valley. In a way it is regrettable Mzilikazi was not allowed to remain in the valley. It is the kind of place that stirs an attachment to the land, especially to the farmer whose livelihood comes from cattle rearing and crop faming.

It was at Kuruman, a London Missionary Society station, where Mzilikazi met the head of the station, Dr. Robert Moffat who advised him to move across the Limpopo to establish a new homeland in Matabeleland, rather than face unending wars with the Boers who in increasing numbers were running away from British colonial misrule in the Cape Colony. It is of historical importance that mention must be made of the fact that when he met Moffat, Mzilikazi was accompanied by his heir apparent, Nkulumane who had been born and named Kanda, only for Moffat to rename him Kuruman, a name that has a fitting sound with Nkulumane, although in the Nguni language the letter "r" is unusual. So, Robert Moffat's Kuruman became Nkulumane, the man who was to become a disputed king when he ascended the throne "before his father's sun had set".

Nkulumane lies buried in the village of Phukeng near the mining city of Rustenburg in the north end of the valley where he settled following his exile from his father's kingdom in Matabeleland. The King was furious and secretly ordered his exile. But some quarters say Nkulumane, like his mother who died at Ntabazinduna with the chiefs who were blamed for his coronation, was taken to the Matopos Hills and executed. This strongly discounts reports that Nkulumane, whose birth name was Kanda, lies buried at Phukeng near the mining city of Rustenburg. This city is not very far from Kuruman where Mzilikazi and his heir to the throne met Dr. Robert Moffat.

A regiment led by a decorated hero, Mbiko kaMadlenya Masuku was ordered to accompany Nkulumane back to Marico Valley. Mbiko was married to one of Mzilikazi's daughters, Zinkabi, who despised her half-brother Lobengula as someone who had "sour saliva". Lobengula succeeded Mzilikazi after the King's death in 1868, and Mbiko and Zinkabi were killed in bloody civil war between the factions of Nkulumane against those of Lobengula. The man who is buried among the Khumalos at Phukeng could be a pretender who worked for a British civil servant in Natal where those who were sent to bring Nkulumane home drew a blank and returned home after satisfying themselves he was not the Nkulumane they were looking for.

There is a popular legend, however, that Nkulumane and his mother were secretly executed and, to give credence to the legend, several leading chiefs were blamed for what Mzilikazi considered to be a treasonous act and the chiefs paid with their lives for it. A hill northeast of Bulawayo got its name, Ntabayezinduna, where the impeached chiefs kept their appointment with death. Nkulumane's mother died with them.

The Nkulumane saga, some say, should be laid to rest, with the established fact that a man who is buried among the Ndebele at Phukeng is generally claimed to be Nkulumane. Phukeng is in the Marico Valley. A man who claimed to be Nkulumane lived in the Bakwena country and established a family, including two sons named Nkume and Basa.

One of the two brothers fathered a son and named him Johannes Ngwalongwalo Khumalo, whose middle name is in recognition of Ngwalongwalo ka Matshobana, Mzilikazi's father. Johannes Ngwalongwalo, who was 76 years old in 2015, still lived in the village of Phokeng with other descendants of Mzilikazi.

Johannes Ngwalongwalo, who in June 2015 was showing signs of declining health, said in an interview he could not return to Bulawayo to claim his great grandfather's right to the crown of the Matabele kingdom.

"The heir to the throne of the Amandebele nation passed from Nkulumane to Lobengula, and I have no right to claim it", he said in an almost whispering but clear voice.

I was, in 2015, privileged to attend an annual all-night commemoration in honour of Nkulumane during which the Khumalo clansmen and their families sat around a flaming log fire overlooking a grave which is marked by a white marble headstone.

During my travel through the area, I marvelled at the great cattle and agricultural land that is Marico Valley. Nothing more than the cruel necessity to look for a new home could have forced Mzilikazi to move from Marico Valley to settle in Matabeleland.

The next phase of Mzilikazi's search for a home was not without strife as wars were fought with the Boers, and indeed with those who succeeded Tshaka. Mzilikazi's last but major war against the Boers came in 1847 with Mzilikazi now settled in the Zambezi Valley with headquarters in Bulawayo. For some time, peace between Mzilikazi and the Boers had been elusive and relations tense until after the 1847 war which led to the first Matabele-Boer Treaty of 1853. Mzilikazi, now settled in his new homeland since 1838, was to live in peace with Boers for the rest of his life. Mzilikazi's flight from Tshaka has an important historical message for the student of history of Southern Africa.

This is particularly important to the present-day generations of the people of the country that in 1980 became Zimbabwe. I mentioned earlier in this narrative the historical fact of Mzilikazi' move away from Marico Valley to avoid war with Boers led by Maritz and Potgieter who, in turn, were fleeing from the British-ruled Cape Colony

There is a popular but dangerous tendency within the ranks of the ruling elite in Zimbabwe. It is that the Matabele – like whites who followed Cecil John Rhodes into the country – are settlers and must return "home" where they came from. As already stated, the Matabele were happy in the Marico Valley but were driven away by other elements as the white man advanced his hegemony driven trek from the Cape Colony. The Boers were not forced by any need to find a home but, like the British, by greed and avarice. It was not greed, avarice or hegemony that forced Mzilikazi to leave Marico Valley, but a cruel necessity to find a home for his people. A group of British colonists later occupied Mashonaland where they were welcomed, and later recruited the local people to join in the white man's invasion of Matabeleland.

It was these same white men who expropriated both Mashonaland and Matabeleland, leaving both the

Mashona and the Matabele without land rights and, in the case of the Matabele, without their cattle as well which were expropriated in a manner that has no parallel in history.

And yet the Mashona, now a military power acquired through their co-operation with white colonists, have never plucked up courage to tell white settlers to return where they came from!

In his book *Sunshine and Storm in Rhodesia* Frederick Courtney Selous has the following to say about them: "When the secret history of the rebellion in Mashonaland comes to be known, I fancy it will be found that it was brought about by the leaders of the Matabele. As for the rising in Mashonaland proving that the native of that country have been very cruelly treated by the whites ..."

What Selous is trying to assert is that the whites did not mistreat the rebelling Mashona. When there is overwhelming historical record that forces of the British South Africa Company threw explosives into caves where the rebelling Mashona were hiding?

But Selous has some extremely unflattering words for the conduct of the Mashona. Denying charges of ill-treatment of the people of Mashonaland, Selous charges "It only shows that the Mashona imagined that they would possess themselves of a vast amount of valuable loot with little danger to themselves, and no fear of punishment". Selous continues: "The kindness or otherwise of the government of the whites would not be likely to weigh with them one way or the other, given their belief in their own power to kill the whites and take possession of their property without fear of retribution".

Let us stop here for moment while we try to unravel this package of meaningless waffling. He charges the people of Mashonaland with being wilful mercenaries who were prepared to kill and possess "loot" with impunity. However, he avoids admitting that the people had every reason to fear retribution because they were in fact blown up with explosives in caves where they were taking refuge.

But if they believed "in their own power to kill the whites and take possession of their property without fear of retribution" why did they fail to demonstrate this power in 1890 when the white man occupied their territory?

Charging that the people believed in themselves, Selous says "that is the crux of the whole question; for one who has lived amongst the various peoples generally known as Mashonas, whose principal characteristics are avarice, cowardice and complete callousness to the suffering of others, will be inclined to doubt that were they governed by an angel from heaven, they would infallibly kill that angel, if his wing feathers were of any value to them, provided that they believed at the same time that the crime might be committed with impunity".

When did the white man make this discovery? When they occupied Mashonaland without a shot or when the people of Mashonaland decided to join the perfidious Matabele in rebellion? The world has been told that the white man occupied Mashonaland to protect the people of Mashonaland. Selous is not alive to explain why the occupation and the rebellion are in such sharp contrast. The waffling above does not tell us either.

Unfortunately, the bastion of tribalism, which has been created in that region does not provide an answer either, and Mashonaland has remained an unassailable comfort zone for the people. It is an apartheid form of government which is formidable in its exclusiveness. Also, common knowledge that the Mashona were historically regarded as those who fled from possible danger at the drop of a fig instead of defending their territory. This earned them the name "Matshona", those who take to their heels at the approach of possible danger. They did not have the courage to defend their own land and the white man corrupted the name "Matshona" to Mashona which has become a source of inextinguishable pride for them.

Moreover, history has recorded that there was a general migration from the south to the north by Bantu tribes during the time when Mzilikazi settled in the Zambezi Valley.

Ten years before Mzilikazi, Mbuzeni (Mpezeni) went through the same valley to settle in Eastern Zambia. History records that Zwangendaba went through the land between Limpopo and the Zambezi to reach Kenya before settling in Nyasaland. There is also the case of Soshangane who settled southeast of Zimbabwe in what became Gazaland. But have the people of Zambia (72 tribes of them) or Malawi ever squealed about the Angoni/Nguni people in their countries? No. This is a lesson for all peace-loving people to observe. Mzilikazi's followers died defending their country against the forces of the Chartered Company coalition with the Mashona. The Matabele, therefore, are in Matabeleland to stay whether their detractors like it or not. The Matabele fought and died defending their own territory and will fight again should their enemies launch another enterprise of genocide against them.

With the signing of the Grobler Treaty in July 1887, relations between the Transvaal Republic and Matabeleland were now poised to develop in the right direction at long last. However, this was reckoned without plans of agents of the Chartered Company who were working to spring a surprise on their opponents by murdering Piet Grobler on his last leg to take residence at Bulawayo as the Republic's first Consul. According to Stanlake Samkange's book, *Origins of Rhodesia*, a mine of information on the early history of the Nguni people, fifty years beginning around 1836, marked the beginning of a scramble for the occupation of the land between the Limpopo and Zambezi rivers, with the Portuguese coming from the east, the Germans from the west, and the British, now having taken Chief Khama's hand and declared Bechuanaland an Imperial Protectorate, competing for territory with Dutch trekkers from the south.

This rivalry between the British and Dutch was later to lead to the Jameson Raid into the Transvaal in 1896 which provided an opportunity, some say, for the Matabele rising against white settlers and the Chartered Company.

The British became the first to sign a Treaty of Agreement with Mzilikazi in 1836 which was signed by Sir Benjamin d'Urban for the United Kingdom and Mncumbata representing Mzilikazi. It was signed on 3 March 1836 and was in 1888 used by Cecil John Rhodes to keep the Boers out of Matabeleland by seeking to discredit the Grobler Treaty.

Between 1847 and 1887 Mzilikazi and his successor Lobengula had entered into a number of treaties of friendship with the Transvaal Republic which could have brought the Matabele nation under the Dutch sphere of influence. These treaties had established the Limpopo River as the southern boundary between Bulawayo and Pretoria, leaving Mzilikazi in peace with the Transvaal until his death in September 1868. The Boers in the Transvaal, for unknown reasons, failed to seize opportunities to take Lobengula's hand of friendship until it was too late to frustrate the British who were granted the Moffat Treaty in 1888, only months after the signing of the Grobler Treaty. The granting of this treaty resulted in a flurry of moves that were designed to discredit the Grobler Treaty, and this led to his tragic and mysterious death for which the British Protectorate of Bechuanaland was blamed.

This happened at Shashi as Grobler – after a great deal of feet-dragging on the part of the Transvaal Republic – was finally moving to become Consul in Bulawayo, six months after the signing of the Grobler Treaty. It took the

Boers 32 years from 1853 when the first of a series of peace treaties with the Matabele was first signed. This indecisiveness on the part of the Transvaal Republic government lost the Boers a number of opportunities which, seized when they occurred, could have changed the course of history of South Africa. In 1888 the British moved to be granted the Moffat Treaty. The British were later granted the Royal Charter to occupy Mashonaland on September 12, 1890, followed by the invasion of Matabeleland in October 1893. The indecisiveness of the South African Republic, it can be argued, led to two tragic events: the murder of Grobler and the subsequent occupation of Mashonaland.

The political and imperial value of Rhodes' move is well known and need no emphasis but it is clear that he spared no money, intrigue, murder and downright lies to keep his rivals out of Matabeleland.

Those employed in this exercise stopped at nothing to accomplish their objectives, as amply manifested by the Rudd Concession, a fraudulent document that led to the impeachment and execution of Paramount Chief Lotshe for allegedly misleading Lobengula about the extent to which the Chartered Company could rely on the concession in its endeavour to occupy the kingdom

Years later, it was discovered that the Rudd Concession did not in fact grant the Chartered Company effective occupation rights of both Matabeleland and Mashonaland but that did not resurrect Lotshe's life. This was also the case with the Moffat Treaty of 1888 and the Royal Charter of 1889.

It is important at this stage to deal with the value of features of the treaties the Boers signed with either Mzilikazi in 1853 or Lobengula in 1887, and subsequently the treaties Lobengula signed with the British.

However, there is a lot to support the view that one-sided though these treaties were, their existence contributed to peace between the Republic and the Matabele Kingdom.

A key omission of these treaties was the absence of provision for mutual defence in the event of one party being attacked by an enemy. This is clearly manifest in the Republic's failure to come to Lobengula's aid when the Pioneer Column marched through his territory on the way to occupy Mashonaland which fell under Lobengula's sphere of influence. It is important that, with the Grobler Treaty established, further examination of the treaty should be undertaken to establish its provisions and terms of reference. It has some glaring limitations especially where mutual reciprocity was concerned. The treaty in the main limited relations between the two nations to hunting in the kingdom, protection of citizens of the Republic who may be resident in the kingdom, and exchange of gifts all of which, it is clear, were expected of Lobengula.

It stipulates:

- *ARTICLE I*

    'There will be everlasting peace and friendship between both parties. No transgression of mutual territories shall have a place."

- *ARTICLE II*

    'The Paramount Chief Lobengula is recognized as an Independent Paramount chief. He will be an ally of the South Africa Republic."

- *ARTICLE III*

> *"The said Chief Lobengula commits himself to provide assistance at all times, whenever he is summoned by the State President or by and officer of the South African Republic to grant any assistance, either with troops or otherwise, to furnish such assistance; and his people shall then have to stand under the command of the commanding officer or lesser officer under him, without he or one of his men showing the least disobedience."*

A notable feature is the absence of any commitment on the part of the Republic to the ideal of mutuality, an important feature that should not be ignored in a similar treaty.

It leaves the reader wondering whether the Republic was not playing the bully against its poorly armed ally in the game of diplomacy! What was the value of a treaty that made no provision for mutual defence in a situation where several parties were scrambling to take Lobengula's Kingdom)?

- ARTICLE IV

  'The Paramount Chief Lobengula shall catch and extradite all criminals that escape from the South African Republic into his territory as shall hence be demanded.

- ARTICLE V

  'The above-said Lobengula shall freely permit each person coming from the Republic with a passport from his Honour, the State President, to hunt and

trade freely, and he will help procure or provide all protection for such hunters, travellers and traders. Such hunters and travellers will have to, however, behave themselves quietly and properly, use no violence, and also not take away anything arbitrarily."

- ARTICLE VI

"If the State President appoints a person to live in the territory of the Paramount Chief Lobengula and, as consul to superintend the subjects of the South African Republic, then such a person shall be provided all necessary protection, for his person as well as for his possessions. He will administer criminal and civil justice over all subjects of the South African Republic. If they should be a civil case between the subjects of the South African Republic and a subject of the above said Paramount Chief Lobengula or another person, then this consul shall also jointly administer the justice."

- ARTICLE VII

"As proof that the State-President of the South African Republic and the Paramount Chief Lobengula approve this treaty, each shall send to the other as soon as possible the following presents,

The State-President of the South African Republic shall send:..

'The Paramount Chief Lobengula shall send:..

With this, I, Lobengula and my council acknowledge this

document as fully approved and marked.

Signed: Paramount Chief Lobengula his **X** mark,

P. J. Grobler,

The undersigned Indunas:

Moluchelu, **X**
Nowcho, **X**
Postochau, **X**

As witness

F. A. Grobler

"Signed at Omchaunien, Matabeleland, on 30 July 1887."

It must be noted that the names of the witnessing chiefs present in this document bear no resemblance to names of the well-known chiefs in Lobengula's kingdom, although it must be accepted this should not detract from the authenticity of the treaty.

However, before one can examine further the value and other attributes of the treaty, it must be compared with the Moffat Treaty which was signed between the British Assistant High Commissioner and Lobengula on 11 February 1888. The Grobler Treaty, as already indicated, had been signed six months earlier, giving the South African Republic more than a head start to bring the Matabele nation under Paul Kruger's sphere of influence.

However, it is not important whether the Matabele came under the South African Republic or the British. What is, is what each contender for friendship with Lobengula was willing to do to promote mutual peace in the region. It will be shown later, for instance, that the British South

Africa Company used John Moffat to get the Moffat Treaty. This was intended to facilitate the granting of the Royal Charter. Both the treaty and the Royal Charter were not intended to prevent invasion of the kingdom.

It is a fact that the Chartered Company was not motivated by any desire to promote peace with Lobengula. The pretensions in this regard were, therefore, designed to mislead. A classic example is the Royal Charter petition.

Available records show that Lobengula's peace overtures were frustrated at every step of the way and this inevitably led to the invasion of Matabeleland in 1893 and the tragic results of a conflict that could have been avoided.

This subject will be dealt with in greater detail later in this book, especially where the British Government is concerned. However, it is noteworthy that the invasion flew in the face of two treaties of friendship between the Imperial Government and the Matabele. But the big lie was that the British South Africa Company occupied Mashonaland and invaded the Matabele kingdom "to protect the poor Mashona" against the Matabele. What had happened to the idea of expanding the British Empire?

However, one must not move on without touching on the missed opportunities on the part of the South African Republic to help forestall the British-Matabele war. Following the Matabele-Boer War of 1847, a verbal peace agreement had been negotiated between Mzilikazi and a group of Boers led by Andries Hendrik Potgieter known to the Matabele by the curious name of "Enteleka". Potgieter was a commandant of the Holland South African Emigrants. The agreement was formalized in Zoutpansberg on 8 January 1853, with Pieter Johannes Potgieter signing for the Republic and Captain Marati for Mzilikazi, witnessed by Chr. J. Rake and D. G. Grobler. Although there are some curious features in this treaty, there is no record that it was ever repudiated.

In fact, Lobengula referred to it in 1888 when the

Grobler Treaty was being challenged by the British authorities as invalid. The treaty can, therefore, be quoted as one of a number of treaties that Mzilikazi and Lobengula entered into with the South African Republic. The 1853 treaty is in fact the legal instrument that established the Limpopo River as the effective boundary between the Matabele Kingdom and the South African Republic.

It is clear, therefore, from this account that the South African Republic failed to seize an opportunity to come to Lobengula's aid when he needed such aid most. Was it the fear of confronting British forces that won the day in this regard or were there other considerations? It is difficult to avoid the conclusion that the Republic's intervention might have delayed or even prevented the war
It took the Republic six months and eleven days for Piet Grobler to take steps to move to Bulawayo to become Consul for his country, only to be fatally wounded in a mysterious skirmish with forces of the British Protectorate of Bechuanaland near Shashi on the last leg of his move to the Matabele capital.

The following is the text of the Moffat Treaty which in due course lost the Republic an opportunity to expand its sphere of influence:

- *'The Chief Lobengula, the ruler of the tribe known as Amandebele, together with Mashona and Makalaka tributaries of the same, hereby agrees to the following articles and conditions:*

Of note is the reference in the preamble of the petition to the Mashona and the Makalaka tributaries.
While the tribe known as the Makalanga became part of Mzilikazi's kingdom, and Mzilikazi ruled the kingdom with Mambo, the Mashona did not become part of the kingdom and Mzilikazi did not usurp any land that belonged to them to make the Mashona his subjects.

This position remained the same under Lobengula. But this should not detract from the fact that Mashonaland was in the Matabele Kingdom's sphere of influence.

- 'That peace and amity will continue forever between Her Britannic Majesty, her subjects and the Amandebele people, and the contracting Chief Lobengula, engages to use his utmost endeavours to prevent any rupture of the same, to cause the strictest observance of this treaty, and so to carry out the treaty of friendship which was entered into by his late father, the Chief Umsiligaas, with the Governor of the Cape of Good Hope, in the year of our Lord 1836'.

The Moffat Treaty therefore reaffirmed the letter and spirit of friendship contained in the d'Urban Treaty of 1836. Lobengula often referred to it to point out his kingdom's desire to live peacefully with Great Britain.

- "It is hereby further agreed by Lobengula, Chief in and over the Amandebele country, with dependences as aforesaid, on behalf of himself and people, that he will refrain from entering into any correspondence or treaty with any foreign state or power to sell, alienate or cede or countenance any sale, alienation or cession of the whole or any part of the said Amandebele country under his chieftainship, or upon any other subject without the previous knowledge and sanction of Her Majesty's High Commissioner for South Africa."

In faith of which I, Lobengula, on my part have hitherto set my hands at Gubulawayo, Amandebeleland, this eleventh day of February, and of Her Majesty's reign the 51st year'.

It is signed by Lobengula with X mark, and J. S. Moffat, witnessed by W. Graham and G. B. van Wyk.

One therefore might wonder why the Chartered Company, which actually sponsored Moffat to obtain the treaty on behalf of the Imperial Government, launched a punitive military expedition against Lobengula.

It is critical to point out that, among other things, this treaty bound the parties to peace and amity forever. It is further noteworthy that even before the ink had dried on the agreed document, Rhodes was already thinking of revisiting his exploits with Lobengula by sending Charles Rudd to seek a concession to facilitate the granting of the Royal Charter that finally cleared the decks for Rhodes to occupy Mashonaland in preparation for the invasion of Matabeleland. It must be noted that the Rudd Concession, the Royal Charter and the Lippert Concession did not authorize invasion or occupation of Matabeleland. What impelled the Chartered Company to invade, after nearly five years of preparation, was the signing of the Victoria Secret Agreement of 14 August 1893. An interesting feature is that the Moffat Treaty, while purporting to be a pact between Her Britannic Majesty and Lobengula, one of its limitations was its failure to make provision for mutual defence in the event of war on either party. It appears these treaties were sought by Europeans to further certain ends, and not mutual defence in the event of an outbreak of war. It must further be observed that the occupation of Mashonaland, let alone the invasion of Matabeleland, was a provocative act that flew in the face of the d'Urban and the Moffat treaties.

Was the omission of a clause for mutual defence a deliberate ploy because it would have put the British South Africa Company on a military collision course with Queen Victoria's government? Was it because while he made threats to declare a Republic in Matabeleland on the lines of the United States of America, Rhodes in fact dreaded war with the Queen because this would have lost him the support of British government representatives in both the Cape of Good Hope and the Protectorate of Bechuanaland? Rhodes needed Sir Hercules Robinson's and Shippard's support to get the Royal Charter. It was Robinson and Shippard who provided a letter of introduction to Moffat to present to Lobengula at the request of Rhodes.

Critical as well, moreover, is that the Imperial Government granted the Chartered Company the Royal Charter believing that it would prevent the invasion of Matabeleland, a move to which Queen Victoria was opposed. The Foreign Office in London was, however, kept in blissful ignorance about Rhodes and the Chartered Company's real plans to invade Matabeleland without unnecessarily precipitating a rupture in relations with Her Majesty's Government.

It, therefore, was not a stroke of luck that prevented such a break at that time but a deliberate strategy to get the Charter through, first of all, using John Moffat instructed by Shippard, supported without compunction, by Sir Hercules Robinson.

One of the chief clauses in the Moffat Treaty stipulates the maintenance of peace and amity between Great Britain and Matabeleland forever, while British representatives on the ground sanctioned the occupation of Mashonaland, a tributary of Lobengula's kingdom, using, not diplomacy but precision arms of war. This conspiracy meant that the Moffat Treaty became just a piece of paper with little if any diplomatic value when Rhodes, by deception, brought it into play. It is also strange that the treaty required Lobengula not to sign any treaty with any other party that might wish to seek such a treaty, without first advising the Imperial Government. This explains why the Chartered Company (and not the Imperial Government) attempted to discredit the Grobler Treaty, and when that failed, Piet

Grobler was confronted by the Bechuanaland Border Police, (alerted by Moffat), and murdered during a skirmish with them.

That episode marked the end of efforts to cultivate diplomatic relations between the Matabele Kingdom and the South African Republic. It would appear the Republic did not want to confront the British South Africa Company in battle for Matabeleland. In that event, was the purpose for which a man lost his life a mere game or design on the part of the Republic to facilitate the exchange of gifts between the two states? It is noteworthy that the Grobler Treaty pays a great deal of emphasis on the protection of citizens of the Republic who might enter the kingdom for hunting purposes. It avoids, like the plague any reference to mutual defence or anything of a military nature. Hunting safaris were the only purpose for which the Grobler Treaty was signed, and Piet Grobler paid with his life for the privilege. What makes this treaty ridiculous is the fact that the South Africa Republic reserved for itself the right to call on Lobengula to provide men for military service under the command of an officer of the Republic!

Let us now look briefly at the notorious Rudd Concession which, though discredited, bought the Chartered Company critical time to hasten the end for the Matabele nation. While its validity was being debated and challenged in South Africa, Rhodes enlisted the support of Sir Hercules to provide a letter of introduction to Lobengula on behalf of Queen Victoria, on whose behalf, Lobengula believed, the concession would promote respect for territorial integrity of the kingdom when, in fact, its purpose was to buy the Chartered Company time to plan its next move. The move involved another time-buying device, the petition for a charter. A point that cannot be over-emphasised is the fact that the Chartered Company did not need a Royal Charter or concession to occupy

Mashonaland or to invade Matabeleland, although the Moffat Treaty describes Mashonaland as a dependency of the Matabele Kingdom. Rhodes and Jameson had other cards up their sleeves. This point will be shown later. As the world now knows, the Rudd Concession was changed to suit Rhodes' designs but eventually shunted to oblivion where all fraudulent documents belong, not even Rhodes' attempt to salvage it with another discredited concession, the Lippert Concession, could save it. However, by the time the Rudd Concession had finally lost its claim to validity, Rhodes had had his Royal Charter granted!

Both the Rudd Concession and the Lippert Concession did not authorize effective occupation of Matabeleland. How then does one explain paramount Chief Lotshe's execution for allegedly misleading Lobengula? He died because of a tragic misunderstanding of the terms of the Rudd Concession by two white missionaries from Inyati Mission who, instead of Charles Helm, were summoned by Lobengula to explain the terms of the Rudd Concession. Helm, who was one of the witnesses to sign the document, was away at the war front somewhere in North Africa. One of the questions that Lobengula asked was 'if the white men found gold in my home, would they dig it?' The answer from the two missionaries was affirmative. That sealed Lotshe's fate. But the granting of the Charter only enabled the British South Africa Company to form what became the Chartered Company. It did not authorize the Chartered Company to effectively occupy the Kingdom. Another important point to remember is that although the Rudd Concession mentioned Mashonaland as part of the ground where mining was to be carried out, the gold was in Matabeleland and the occupation of Mashonaland was done through a route outside of Matabeleland.

Why was it important for Rhodes to have a Charter?

This point is explained elsewhere in the book but suffice it to say Rhodes was running out of money to finance his expedition and only a Chartered Company could attract more investors to join and this is how Alfred Beit came in with his millions.

However, the occupation of Mashonaland ensured that the direct route through Bulawayo to Mount Hampden was avoided because it would have led to a violation of the Kingdom's territorial integrity. It must be observed that the idea of acquiring both the Lippert and Rudd concessions by the Chartered Company was to fortify the idea of what could have been the effective occupation of Matabeleland. At the risk of belabouring this point, let me repeat the point that the two concessions and the Royal Charter did not grant the company effective occupation of Matabeleland. I am emphasizing this point to show that perfidious Lobengula did not open the floodgates to let white settlers take his kingdom. In contrast, the chiefs of Mashonaland did the opposite: welcomed the Pioneer Column and these same chiefs went further by allowing their people to be recruited by the settlers to invade Matabeleland. The enormous political dimension of this development was exploited by the Pioneer Column in a divide-and-rule strategy which professed that the divine purpose to occupy Mashonaland and invade Matabeleland, was to "protect the poor Mashona" against the Matabele.

History has shown that the people of Mashonaland paid a high price for their poor judgment of the situation. The British demonstrated during the 1897 uprising that no crime was too heinous for them to commit against even the Mashona, as the Matabele had always known it. In due course the colonialists went further and expropriated land that belonged to the Mashona. And this again, is in sharp contrast to Mzilikazi and Lobengula's policy pertaining to the land of the Mashona.

However, reference must be made to the time it took for Charles Dunnell Rudd, Rochford Maguire and Francis Thompson to get Lobengula to give them the concession. It was like extracting a deeply embedded tooth. The trio arrived in Bulawayo on 20 September 1888 to be met by John Moffat who soon arranged for them to appear before the king. What is important at this stage is not so much the trio's arrival and reception, but rather, the fact that it was to be another eight months before they were granted a signed document.

It had been a long wait since the signing of the Moffat Treaty but not long enough to allow Piet Grobler the South African Republic envoy to settle down in Bulawayo to entrench diplomatic relations between his country and the Matabele Kingdom. The failure of Grobler's mission to the kingdom, moreover, marked the beginning of the end of the proposals of the Moffat Treaty for peace and amity between the kingdom and the United Kingdom.

On 12 September 1890, the Pioneer Column of the BSAC raised the British flag on Cecil Square in Salisbury, followed on 3 October 1893 by the invasion of Matabeleland against the letter and the spirit of the Moffat Treaty. The political and tragic ramifications of the occupation and invasion will be given due account in succeeding chapters of this book. In the meantime, a close examination must be made of the Grobler Treaty that should have prevented the occupation (or at least delayed it) of Mashonaland and the invasion of Matabeleland, which triggered the war against Lobengula that need not have come about. There were treaties of friendship with the British which should have forestalled the outbreak of war. Prevention of war, despite these treaties, was not possible because the Imperial Government was secretly in league with the Chartered Company and the treaties only served to mislead and betray Lobengula.

CHAPTER 2

BOERS OUTRACED BY THE BRITISH

FROM the day on 8 January 1853 when Pieter Johannes Potgieter and Captain Marati signed a pact of friendship known as the "Silkaas Treaty", establishing the Limpopo River as the boundary between Matabeleland and the South African Republic, a whole new world was opened for the Boers to expand their sphere of influence by taking Matabeleland under their hand. With the Transvaal joining forces with the Matabele against the British South Africa Company, Cecil John Rhodes' expansion into the land between the Two Rivers would have seen the Boers, then led by, running ahead of the Chartered Company by Andries Hendrik Potgieter many years. A military pact of Boers and the Matabele would have been enough to frustrate the Englishman's designs on Matabeleland.

The Matabele and the Republic fighting against the British posed a formidable force to withstand the enemy. Is it not the Boers who initiated the laager defences and often used them to stand up to the British during the 1896 Jameson Raid and other times when the two sides faced each other in conflict? Was it not the Boers who prevented British colonists from gobbling up the whole of South Africa for the British Empire?

Was it not the Boers who defeated the British during the ill-conceived Jameson Raid? And yet they failed to capitalize on the prevailing peace with Mzilikazi for 20 years.

It is clear that Paul Kruger who was president during the critical time of relations with Lobengula must take the blame for the lost opportunity, but the world will probably never know why he saw no merit in it even as he and Lobengula exchanged gifts to cement their relations. By the time the Republic finally moved, it was too late to thwart British contenders for Matabeleland.

But the purpose of recalling the events of that important period in the history of Southern Africa, the focus of my comments is, as already shown, more on the terms of the Grobler Treaty, rather than apportioning blame on any one of the power players in the Republic. The failure to seize the opportunity has now become so much water under the bridge.

One of the limitations of the Grobler Treaty is the absence of reciprocity in the treaty to provide for mutual defence in the event of Lobengula being attacked by a third party. The treaty provided for the Republic to call on Lobengula to provide his army to defend the Republic should the republic be attacked by a mutual enemy.

Why was the treaty so one-sided as to render it a farce? The treaty for all intents and purposes provided a feature for strong and friendly ties and, due to its force Mzilikazi lived in peace with the Republic for the rest of his life.

Why was the Republic's failure to come to Lobengula's defence when faced with the British the only way to show the Republic's thanks and appreciation of peace with Mzilikazi?

And yet when the territorial integrity of Matabeleland under Lobengula was being violated by the Pioneer Column, the Republic offered no assistance to Lobengula. Of course, the question remains as to whether Lobengula asked for such assistance. But does not the mutual value of a treaty dictate that one party or the other should offer assistance to a beleaguered ally? And of course, this question begs another: Did the Republic offer assistance to an ally who had on at least two occasions sent gifts of ivory to Paul Kruger to strengthen friendly relations which had been developing since after the 1847 war with Mzilikazi?

The climax of the Republic's lethargic relations with Lobengula came when Piet Grobler, the Republic's consul designate was murdered while moving to take residence at Bulawayo in 1888. Was it not diplomatically expedient, at the very least, for the Republic to show its anger by offering Lobengula assistance in 1890 even though the king did not ask for it, which many observers would consider strange?

It is interesting that the Pioneer Column set off to occupy Mashonaland from Tuli, a spitting distance from Shashi the scene of Grobler's murder. It is further noteworthy that it was John Moffat, the man who tried to prove that Lobengula had not signed any treaty with Grobler, who alerted Khama's Mounted Police of 300 men to intercept Grobler, leading to his tragic murder. This is food for thought for the Republic's history scholars. The failure by the Republic to reciprocate, however, sapped the value of the treaty at a time when it should have been strengthened.

It is said history repeats itself and, with this state in mind, let us look at another treaty that fell by the wayside, this time due to duplicity of other forces that were arrayed against the Matabele nation.

On 3 March 1836 Chief Mncumbata, on behalf of Mzilikazi, signed the Treaty of Agreement with Sir Benjamin d'Urban, Governor of the Cape of Good Hope. The treaty among other things, committed Mzilikazi to be "a faithful friend and ally of the Cape Colony, maintain peace, to protect white people who, with his consent, visited or were resident in his country". For his part, Sir Benjamin agreed to accept Mzilikazi and the Matabele people as friends of the British Government. The Governor was to consider Mzilikazi's request for a white official to be resident in Matabeleland. In addition, Mzilikazi agreed to abstain from war.

It is important to note that after he became king, Lobengula – for years now beleaguered by hostile forces led by Cecil John Rhodes - often in a desperate bid to be left alone, referred to this treaty of friendship with the Cape Colony.

It is unlikely, therefore, that Rhodes had forgotten the existence of this treaty of friendship. In fact, it will be remembered that Rhodes often castigated Queen Victoria for refusing to sanction the invasion of Matabeleland.

Queen Victoria – for her credit – saw the duplicity of invasion in the face of a treaty with the Matabele whose unambiguous terms could not be ignored by a party that subscribed to honourable conduct.

Of historical importance is the welter of evidence that Lobengula, like his father before him, did all he could to promote peaceful co-existence with his neighbours, and was in fact not a sabre-rattling, blood-minded savage that his enemies told the world he was. It will be shown in subsequent chapters of this book that the propaganda war against him duped the world and bought Rhodes blood time that led to the commission of war crimes in the name of the so-called white civilization.

CHAPTER 3

A POINT OF NO RETURN

WHEN the Pioneer Column occupied Mashonaland on 12 September 1890, with this territory still under Lobengula's sphere of influence, the countdown to the invasion of Matabeleland in October 1893 began, to be followed by tragic events for the people of Matabeleland. A great deal of propaganda that held out Lobengula as a wilful and atrocious savage to be smashed, raged in the western world to justify the invasion. Frantically working to prevent hostilities, Lobengula was overwhelmed by the forces that were arrayed against him. While telling the world of its peaceful intentions across the Limpopo, the British South Africa Company, on the other hand, went full throttle to prepare and arm itself for the invasion. And, strangely, the Imperial Government watched like a disinterested spectator.

The infamous Rudd Concession was granted on 30 October 1888, nearly a year after the signing of the Moffat Treaty of "peace and amity" between Lobengula and the British Government, followed by the granting of the Royal Charter on 29 October 1889. The presented reasons for the petition for a Charter included the promotion of trade and commerce, and the improvement of the moral and material well-being of the native tribes. That may sound plausible to British ears, but it was a calculated insult to the Matabele. Why should moral and material well-being of the victims of colonialism be measured by the standard of the Chartered Company or that of the British for that matter? Material wellbeing when the motive was to rob the people of their land, cattle and launch a wanton plunder of mineral resources of the kingdom? It is crystal clear the Chartered Company was involved in a sinister game of justification while actively involved in the pursuit of subterfuge to be granted a Royal Charter.

The Company and the Imperial Government were together involved in a make-believe exercise on a grand scale which on 29 October 1889 saw Queen Victoria granting the Charter with the following as its principal objects:

(a) The working of concessions, "so far as they are valid"; (However, the Company at this stage or any other stage did not hold a valid concession to enter Matabeleland but was actively preparing to invade the Kingdom).

(b) To secure other concessions subject to the approval of the Secretary of State; (contrary to that, the Secretary of State was not Lobengula or his proxy to be expected to approve the granting of concessions to enter Matabeleland).

(c) To preserve peace and order; (The only threat to peace was the Chartered Company).

(d) To abolish the slave trade and domestic slavery; (The slave trade and domestic slavery was a product of the invasion).

(e) To prevent the sale of intoxicants to natives; (The sale of intoxicants was again a product of invasion).

(f) In the administration of justice to consider carefully native laws and customs, especially with regard to rights of property; (Justice and native laws were ignored by the Chartered Company after invasion).

(g) To seek and act upon the advice of the

Imperial authorities. (Such advice was in fact never sought and the need was ignored by the Company after the Charter was granted. The Royal Charter therefore was nothing but a time-buying device for the Company while the Imperial Government believed it would prevent the invasion of Matabeleland).

It is clear, therefore, that once the charter was granted, the Chartered Company, in fact, failed to honour almost all the above-named pledges. That is except slavery among the natives, with tragic results for the people of Matabeleland.

Moreover, such failure exposed the Imperial Government to a possible profound national embarrassment, especially where it concerned British expectations that granting of the Royal Charter would prevent the invasion of Matabeleland.

The failure by the Chartered Company to honour fundamental principles of its petition to secure a Charter, granted ostensibly to protect, among others, some native interests under threat from the Petitioners themselves. It also made the British Government appear to be a willing partner in an armed expedition which, as King Lobengula was later moved to describe it, "to rob me of my people and country".

The land robbery and dispersal of the Africans was given the Royal Seal of the Imperial Government in 1919 when the decision of the Privy Council was published and became the law under the authority of the Imperial Government.

The decision included the rejection or dismissal of the Nyamande Petition for the restoration of the Matabele Kingdom. This petition also sought the declaration of what had become Matabeleland, a British protectorate. As far as the Imperial Government was concerned the Matabele Kingdom and its people had become defunct and their well-being forgotten. The people had been disarmed and the next time the question of self-determination should have been broached was in 1979 when the British Government finally faced a different set of circumstances that precluded the Matabele altogether from the Lancaster House Conference.

I refer at length to the Lancaster House shenanigans later in this narrative. The British Government then faced the so-called nationalists while pleading loss of memory concerning Lobengula's children and the Nyamande Petition. It is my argument that the contrived loss of memory in this regard was part of a Grand Plan to obliterate the existence of the Matabele Kingdom from recorded history.

The British Government found itself ambivalent and walking a tightrope between the interests of the Chartered Company and those of the natives and it chose to support enemies of the native peoples of the two territories of what became Southern Rhodesia. The situation had in 25 years of colonial and imperial free play become a fait accompli so much that the British Government could only undo it, if it wanted to undo the damage at all, by military intervention which was unthinkable. Great Britain has never been known to resort to gunboat diplomacy against its citizens, especially against its own subjects in a foreign country. The exception was in Northern Ireland. British intervention in the province was in support of unionists against republicans. The rationale was that the republicans were not Englishmen.

In perfidious Matabeleland, both the Imperial Government and the Chartered Company were arrayed against the kingdom which did not roll out the red carpet to allow effective occupation of the territory by the Company the British Government, and any military intervention as option was, therefore, out of the question.

It was so even though the tradition of British Honour and Justice were being violated with so much impunity. (Did I hear someone accusing me of being crazy for daring to mention military intervention?). I am only angry that my people were treated so shoddily while the Imperial Government watched disinterestedly.

Even then Rhodes did threaten damnation which he said would lead to a declaration of a Republic and that, under the British legal system, would have been an overt declaration of war with the Imperial Government. Rhodes did, however, warn Queen Victoria to stop meddling. If war broke out between his forces and those of the Imperial Government, he said, the result would make the lives of the natives she was trying to protect worthless by comparison. Queen Victoria suffered cold feet and let the dishonour and injustice, coupled with considerations of race, run their full course.

However, Rhodes was prepared to use the devastating Maxim machine guns and artillery against the Queen's forces! These are the same weapons which the Chartered Company used against the Matabele warriors in 1893. But the land question simmered for many years after the end of the 1893 war, and after the Crown won the land case in 1919 against all three other claimants and a new phase in the dispute was reached. Even then, the British Government could do precious little to allay native fears, only pretending that the dispossessed victims potentially stood to benefit more than all other parties whose claims lay before the Privy Council.

Further examination of British promises will show that the Imperial Government, in fact, did nothing to protect natives' interests in the interim. When time came to surrender Southern Rhodesia to a responsible authority in 1919, it became clear it had to be a white settler government. The conspiracy between the Chartered

Company and the Imperial Government was unfolding in its horrendous and devastating effect, whose effects are still being felt today, with the Matabele the greatest losers.

The publication in 1919 of the Privy Council Report bought the Imperial Government time to prepare the ground to surrender native land to a responsible government without, at the time, admitting that a white settler government was ear-marked for the honour.

It can, however, be stated now, without any hesitation, that Imperial Government expectations regarding native benefits in the form of land, in fact, amounted to self-delusion - a pipe dream which was never realised or ever intended to be realised. It was the pronouncement that the native stood to gain incalculably from the decision of the Privy Council to surrender the land to the British Monarchy.

This is due to the fact that, with the Chartered Company losing its claim before the Privy Council, the Imperial Government became the owners of the land in Matabeleland and Mashonaland and, against all expectations, failed to protect native interests. It was, therefore, a matter of time before the Crown surrendered the land to the next authority which, as already stated, could only be that of white settlers. How then were the dispossessed natives expected to benefit under a hostile and opportunistic white settler regime? The Imperial Government was not concerned about the welfare of the African people, with its only concern being that another African jewel should be added to the British Empire. While this was immoral, what happened to the much-vaunted British honour and justice? Were the natives entitled to justice? No. Instead the natives found themselves faced with a formidable tripartite coalition led by the Imperial Government with the interest of the Chartered Company and a growing white settler community uppermost in the mind of the coalition. Had the Privy Council ruled in favour of Africans as the owners of the land, Lobengula's kingdom could not have been declared defunct. However, such declaration was in the view of the Imperial Government a trivial matter to be ignored or forgotten when independence negotiations with nationalists opened. I will elaborate later why the nationalists were chosen for this honour, against the interests of other parties.

The very fact that the Privy Council ruled against the kingdom is a clear indicator the government of the territory could not revert back to Lobengula's children. But the Privy Council decision declared that the British Crown had succeeded Lobengula. This meant that the Crown, therefore, held the land in trust for Lobengula's people! There is a conflict here between this assertive ruling and the Crown's failure to protect native interests in the five-year interim leading to responsible government that followed in 1923. The only possible protection was to grant Matabeleland a protectorate status. The imperial Government, therefore, sacrificed native interests on the altar of race-based and evil expediency. This was to prepare the way for a racist white settler government five years before it became the Administration in Rhodesia. It will be shown in succeeding pages that all efforts by Lobengula's children to have their kingdom restored were rudely rejected. The Imperial Government, with its formidable authority, was unwilling to seize the opportunity to grant the territory a protectorate status while it held the reins of responsible government in Matabeleland.

The question of a protectorate will be dealt with at some length in the book, and it will become clear to the reader that the Matabele were denied the protection for no other reason than that they had opposed invasion of their kingdom by Englishmen, a good number of whom were killed during the hostilities. By December 1894, hired mercenaries had since the end of the war in December 1893 carved up 21 million acres of prime native land for themselves, without the Imperial Government using that formidable power and authority to intervene. But the Imperial Government would not intervene on the side of the disposed because in the view of the British Government colonialism was a sacrosanct mission to be pursued at the expense of Africans.

So, what was the purpose of replacing the Chartered Company administration if not to address the questionable circumstances that the Company had created?

The usurpation of Matabeleland had been predetermined for the Chartered Company under the secret agreement signed by Leander Starr Jameson on 14 August 1893 as an incentive to invade the Kingdom. The Chartered Company would only go to war with the Matabele, rather than renege on its promises to the hired invaders covered by that Secret Agreement which will be shown later in this book.

But by what arrangement had the natives lost their land to the Company to be expected by the Imperial Government to accept whatever was left of it? It was due to the hopelessness of the situation that led to the 1896 uprising which was smashed by the Chartered Company using a war of attrition which forced the uprising Matabele forces to accept peace with the Chartered Company in November 1897 under abject conditions. The disarmament of the Matabele Warriors sealed the process of dispossession. In the scorched earth policy applied by General Frederick Carrington, the people's cattle and stored grains were destroyed to force them into unconditional surrender. There was no peace treaty, no truce or armistice signed by the warring sides.

They were, in addition, denied their inalienable right to prepare land for the season's crops. If this was not a drive to exterminate them, then when does extermination begin when the people were being starved to death and their remaining cattle destroyed?

I have said I am angry because of the manner in which the people of Matabeleland were treated. The British can dismiss my anger as an emotional outburst with no lasting consequences. But its consequences, which have not died with the passage of time, are purely retrospective, obligating the British Government - indeed the British public - to revisit the shameful expediency of their failure to protect native interests while at the same time the British Government pretended that justice was their concern. When the Matabele kingdom was declared by the Privy Council to have become defunct, nothing was put in place to ensure that native land rights were protected. Did the people also become defunct? Did the human factor also become defunct? Or was the idea merely to relegate them to the gutters of colonialism created by Rhodes and company, whichever was the worst?

I am angry because of the accolade that Cecil John Rhodes received, justifying the commission of war crimes that began with the October 1893 invasion of Matabeleland, crimes which have never been investigated, let alone condemned because the victims were not white men. They were not English men, women and children and, therefore, were expendable without questions being asked. This was the British honour and justice that was being sung across the globe with supporting spectators cheering.

One cannot recall these episodes without getting extremely angry because the plight of the people of Matabeleland in the commission of two genocides against them in a century, in which the hand of the British Government is visible, has not been acknowledged by the perpetrators.

The failure to acknowledge the wrong-doing and condemn the Chartered Company for committing war crimes can only be due to the fact that the people of Great Britain would suffer unprecedented embarrassment and the nation's so-called armour of honour and justice dented. In these circumstances, therefore, why is Great Britain's much vaunted and peculiar honour and justice still being proclaimed from the hilltop?

The fact that the people of Matabeleland fought and killed Britons while defending their country deserves an apology from the people of the United Kingdom.

But British concerns are to present to the world a national image unimpaired by bloody scandals caused by their unprecedented cruel and callous treatment of natives in a bid to build the British Empire. Let us at this point consider the value of the seven clauses of the Charter to establish the extent to which it could be implemented to prejudice the people of Matabeleland, exposing them to untold injustices and bloodshed.

Clause (a) proposes the working of concessions "so far as they are valid". It can be stated emphatically that the Company at the critical time held no valid concessions justifying the granting of the Royal Charter. The Rudd Concession which preceded the petition for a Charter was not only flawed but had also been repudiated by Lobengula who demanded the return of the original document. He never got it until the forces of plunder drove him into exile where he died. That cleared the ground and left the colonist to justify their evil designs.

The British Government, therefore, was grossly ill-advised to grant the Charter in the face of both the Moffat Treaty of Friendship which was being violated and the discredited Rudd Concession. The Imperial Government was aware that the Rudd Concession had limited, if any legal force. But in fairness to Queen Victoria, it must be conceded that the decision to grant the petition was compromised by servants of Her Majesty's Government on the ground who became double agents working for the Company as well. There is also enough evidence that some of the Queen's advisers in the United Kingdom itself were shareholders or potential shareholders in the Chartered Company.

Presuming, therefore, that there was ever any intention to dismiss the petition, this seriously impaired the judgment of those who had to make the final decision. Distance also played a critical role in the matter, with the right hand of proceedings of state acting unknowingly about what the left hand was doing.

When Queen Victoria in her telegram to Lobengula quoted London-based directors of the Chartered Company as assuring the Matabele that the Company had peaceful designs in Matabeleland, no one in London, it would appear, knew that the Company was acting aggressively to promote war with Lobengula on the ground. Overall, however, it was the question of race which determined the fate of the petition against the best interest of the people of Matabeleland. The fear of a possible public opinion backlash must also have influenced the decision. Rhodes had become *The Colossus* of, not only London's financial life, but also as Prime Minister of the Cape Colony.

It can be said, therefore, that the mood in Downing Street was not without consideration of power political fears of the moment as Rhodes drove a promising colonial expedition to add land mass and wealth to the British Empire, using all means possible and his ill- gotten money for the glory of the best race (the British considered themselves so) that God placed on the face of the earth!

Personally, Queen Victoria was doing her level best to avoid anything that threatened the wellbeing and the best interest of the Matabele people, but the solution of the land question was left to posterity to fix.

But once responsible government was installed in 1923 there was no one either in Southern Rhodesia or the United Kingdom willing to do anything about the land problem that affected Africans. It took 77 years for a revolution in the year 2000 to sweep away white land rights in a stunning land reform move by the black apartheid regime led by the incorrigible Robert Mugabe to repair some of the damage. Did this revolution fix the land imbalance for the benefit of all the people of Zimbabwe? The answer is an emphatic No because the ruling party considers the black people of Matabeleland as settlers who must be driven out of the country using all manner of means to accomplish this goal.

These means were led by a genocidal operation against the Matabele which was launched as the country celebrated its first anniversary of independence. The genocide was followed by a plethora of discriminatory practices against the people of Matabeleland across the entire social and political fabric of the nation, whose principle continues to be applied to this day. The only authority that should have worked out an equitable land distribution was the Imperial Government and the only meaningful thing for it to do to accomplish this end was to grant Matabeleland a protectorate status to restore the monarchy.

But what happened in 1923 was just a coma in a design which was calculated to deny the Matabele their natural rights for all time. The final results of this strategy began to unfold in 1979 when the British Government finally struck the last nail in the coffin in which the interests of the Matabele had been lying since the advent of responsible government. This was accomplished by excluding King Lobengula's children from the Lancaster House Conference. As the world knows, this was the culmination of Great Britain's long-awaited king-making exercise to ensure that the so-called defunct Matabele kingdom became a thing of the past for all time. How this process was accomplished is explained in greater detail later in the book.

Morally, the Imperial Government had as much obligation or responsibility to be concerned about the welfare of the subjugated Matabele as it had the responsibility to ensure the welfare of other interests. The policy of the Imperial Government, however, was essentially sectional and driven by racial considerations.

This means that morality, justice and honour were not part of the political and commercial mix of the land question in 1919 and the rights of the natives were sacrificed in a grand betrayal by the Imperial Government to which the Privy Council handed the land in both territories of what became Rhodesia. Africans had, with the decision of the Privy Council, become outsiders in a race-based colonial triangle to rob them of their land. The 25-year build-up to the 1919 Privy Council decision made sure that, when the time came, the natives were not consulted and those like Nyamande who petitioned for restoration of the Matabele monarchy were not only ignored but were also quarantined away from the people. What complicated the land issue is the fact that there were too many forces with vested interest at play for the matter to be fixed and not one of them gave regard to interests of the African people.

This posture of the Imperial Government policy had long been cultivated by the divided loyalty of the servants of the Imperial Government on the ground. Rhodes had ensured that he had the support of key figures representing the British Government in South Africa to get him, first, the Moffat Treaty in the name of the Imperial Government, secondly, the Royal Charter. Until it was fully discredited as a flawed document the Rudd Concession also added to Rhodes' fortunes in no small measure. The reader, however, should understand that neither the Royal Charter nor the Rudd Concession or the Lippert Concession for that matter, authorized the Chartered Company to enter Matabeleland in order to occupy Mashonaland which was part of Lobengula's sphere of influence. This explains why the Pioneer Column left Fort Tuli and went eastward until they reached a point beyond what later became the Jameson Line before turning north to establish camp in Fort Victoria. It was from that parallel route from Fort Tuli which ensured that the Pioneer Column did not set foot in the territory under King Lobengula's effective occupation.

Since the Pioneer Column's final destination was Mount Hampden but they ended up in Salisbury, their most direct route to both destinations, from the British Protectorate of Bechuanaland, was to go through Bulawayo. But the Pioneer Column deviated away from that direct route and this fact cannot be over-emphasized for the benefit of those who persistently and hysterically accuse Lobengula of selling his own country to the colonialist for a bowl of sugar. Nothing explains Lobengula's position on land more forcefully and conclusively than the Baines Concession of November 1876. The following is the full text of that document which is recorded in the book *The Chartered Millions* by John H. Harris. There is no evidence that this policy of the kingdom was ever substituted.

- *"In making this grant I, Lobengula do not alienate from my kingdom this or any other portion of it; but reserve intact the sovereignty of my dominion, and Mr. Baines engaged on behalf of said Company not to make any claim contrary or injurious to my right as sovereign of the country, but recognize my authority as king, and to apply to me for such protection as he might require, and I engaged to grant such protection to Mr. Baines as should enable him to enjoy all lawful and proper use of the privileges granted him by me; and I also certify that when in November of the same year, 1876.*

> - Mr. Baines asked me what tribute or payment he should make me in return for said privileges, I declined to name any such sum, but left it to the judgment of Mr. Baines to make me annually, on behalf of the said Company, such present as might seem proper to him and acceptable to me. Among the Matabele the verbal promise of the king has always been regarded as sufficient guarantee, and many white men now enjoy privileges in virtue of grants made by my father, Umzelegazi, which I regard as binding on me".

This statement cannot be more explicit regarding Lobengula's sovereignty and rights and privileges of those who sought such privileges or rights. The Baines Concession was later acquired by the Chartered Company from the Baines Group (before the granting of the Royal Charter) to fortify the idea of entering Lobengula's Kingdom to establish effective occupation. It will be noted that the letter and spirit of the Baines Concession were so clearly against the effective occupation designs of the Chartered Company that the world was kept ignorant about its existence. The following is a statement by the British Foreign and Colonial Office concerning what had become known as the Rudd- Rhodes Concession after the original Rudd Concession was acquired by the Chartered Company. The statement was provoked by Lobengula's denunciation of the Rudd Concession and his demand that the original document be returned to him.

The Foreign Office statement runs:

"Lord Salisbury is doubtless aware that the British South Africa Company has found itself hitherto somewhat embarrassed by the fact, on which those opposed to it were not disinclined to dwell, that the "Rudd Concession" obtained from Lobengula in 1888 did not in terms of purport to grant more than mining rights in his territories, and that therefore it had but an imperfect

right, if any right at all, to grant such titles to Immovable property as were necessary for the development of a civilized community", said the Foreign Office.

All this waffling by the Foreign Office is British euphemism for saying the Rudd Concession did not grant the Chartered Company the right to effectively occupy both Matabeleland and Mashonaland. The people who granted the right to occupy Mashonaland are the local chiefs while Lobengula refused to open the floodgates to colonial occupation of his kingdom. Going through the motions of seeking the concession, the Charter and acquiring two other concessions, was therefore a time-buying device while the Company was getting ready to invade. That readiness was reached with the signing of the Secret Agreement on 14 August 1893, nearly seven years after the signing of the Rudd Concession.

If there is still any lingering doubt among readers about the value of these concessions, the author is not obliged to give further light on the subject.

The reader should note that it took nearly five years from November 29, 1889, when the Royal Charter was granted ostensibly to promote peaceful designs in Matabeleland, to October 1893 when invasion actually began. But once the Charter was granted, the Company became belligerent and defiant of the Imperial Government when it insisted that peace negotiations with Lobengula had to be done through the High Commissioner's office. With all those flawed instruments to occupy the territory, the Company felt that it no longer needed the co-operation of the High Commissioner and had to go it alone using the Secret Agreement as its "legal" instrument to invade, much to the embarrassment of the Imperial Government. Neither the Imperial Government nor its successors have ever condemned this defiance of authority by the Company, proving beyond any doubt that the Imperial Government was behind scenes working with the Chartered Company in its hostile designs on Matabeleland.

The failure to condemn the Company led to the unthinkable: The Imperial Government subsequently approved the invasion through the issuing of those notorious Matabeleland Orders in Council which unlawfully dispossessed the natives of all land and other possessions.

If the British people were not shamed as a result of this episode in the history of the British Empire, perhaps it is not too late to tell them they should have been. This episode became the first open manifestation of the Imperial Government's hitherto stealth support and involvement in the Grand Plan to rob the natives of their land and its mineral endowment. The second stage was reached 25 years later in 1919 when the British Monarchy became the custodian of the stolen land. This blew the cover from the whole deception that had been put in place way back in 1836 when Great Britain and Mzilikazi signed the first treaty of friendship.

History has recorded that the British Government paid the Chartered Company 20 million pounds sterling for its invasion of Matabeleland and occupation of Mashonaland. This happened when administration of the territories was surrendered to the Responsible Government in 1923. It is important to note that the British Government accepted the principle for its payment to cover costs that the Chartered Company had incurred during its occupation of the two territories. How much did the British Government pay the natives for the robbery of their land and natural resources?

An unavoidable question is: why was it necessary for the British taxpayer to be burdened with the cost of invasion and occupation of the two territories by a commercial undertaking that had for 25 years been selling stolen native land to promote investment fortunes for its members? The answer, of course, is quite simple: The

Imperial Government had a vested interest in the colonial expedition because it added more land mass and mineral wealth to the British Empire. This is how white settlers established title to the land that was eventually taken away from them through a revolution.

This establishes an incontestable obligation on the part of the United Kingdom Government to repair the material damage which was suffered by the people of Matabeleland as a result of the invasion of which the Imperial Government approved through the two Matabeleland Orders in Council already recorded elsewhere in this book. Can the conscience of the British people be pricked to impel them to accept and be willing to consider whether there is still room to repair the damage that was inflicted by their kith and kin on the people of Matabeleland? The people of Matabeleland demand reparations which were stalled and postponed at the Privy Council Conference in 1919 when pretentious promises were made to the people but were negated by the Chartered Company and the Privy Council and, therefore, remain unfulfilled.

Let us return to the subject of the Charter.

Clause (b) of the petition for a Charter was dangled as a carrot to persuade the Secretary of State that he was dealing with honourable men. It is stated in clause (c) that part of the objects of the Charter was to preserve peace and order in Matabeleland. When there was no war and turmoil in the kingdom? Who had disturbed peace before the invasion?

Who is saying there was no peace and order in Matabeleland before the Chartered Company invaded the kingdom? How then could the Crown grant the Charter because the Company promised to preserve peace in Matabeleland when the only threat to peace was posed by the Chartered Company? The Royal Charter was granted and signed on 29 November 1889, with the invasion of Matabeleland coming on 3 October 1893, who maintained peace and order in Matabeleland before the invaders moved in to overrun the kingdom, ignoring the provisions of the Royal Charter? It is curious that the Imperial Government did not question the hidden motive and dismiss the petition.

It must be pointed out that the Charter did not, in fact, confer on the Company authority to enter the territory of Matabeleland because the Imperial Government had no power to confer such authority. The kingdom was a sovereign state and stuck to its guns to keep colonists off its territory. A point to be remembered is that Lobengula did not seek to eject the colonists from Mashonaland which was under the kingdom's sphere of influence.

In clause (d), however, the far-fetched object was the abolishment of slave trade and domestic slavery in Matabeleland. It is universally acknowledged that the emergence of slavery in kingdom was an aftermath of the war and that trade in intoxicants became a social evil with the advent of the so-called free trade. Slavery in Matabeleland was introduced by the colonists.

In clause (e) the petitioners sound like someone proffering what those who had to decide the fate of the petition wanted to hear! There was no widespread distribution of intoxicants to warrant a Royal Charter to reduce the prevalence of intoxicants or outlaw distribution of the substance. The petition should have been thrown out.

To what degree did the presence of intoxicants pose a security threat to the kingdom? The British Monarchy should have raised that question when determining the validity or rationale of the petition. Queen Victoria's government, however, decided to grant a private company the authority to become a policeman in Matabeleland.

The Company in clause (f) gives the impression that there was no fair administration of justice and the respect for native laws and customs under Lobengula, requiring intervention of the Company with its big guns! Did it forget it was about to sign a Secret Agreement with mercenaries to invade Matabeleland, and launch a massive expropriation of native lands and cattle? It is amazing indeed that the Company proposed under clause (g) to seek and act upon the advice of the Secretary of State.

This reflected honourable intent on the part of the petitioners when in actual fact their intention was to buy time until they were ready to invade and rob the people of their land and livestock. Lobengula, as it will be shown, was not fooled by these moves as he watched every step by the Company to invade his country. But the British Government, as reflected in the following dispatch from the High Commissioner still believed war could be averted.

"You (Moffat) can tell the king from me I have no intention of invading his country or of dragging him into war", declared Queen Victoria. This declaration is meaningless and unconvincing when it is clear those who wanted to drag Lobengula into war were the Chartered Company and their partners the Imperial Government. Had the queen lost control of her own government?

According to John Harris in his book *The Chartered Millions*, the Queen quoted the following Chartered Company solemn declaration made as recently as 1892, less than a year before the war to justify her standpoint:

"It is never to be forgotten that the policy of the Company, unlike that of expeditions in other parts of Africa, has been to occupy peacefully under treaties with natives and not by force". But the opposite was being planned for Matabeleland, not by the Queen's government but the Chartered Company. It will take some convincing that the United Kingdom government was not aware of moves to invade. What did the Imperial Government do to prevent invasion? And why did the Queen speak for the Company?

Queen Victoria was actually repeating declarations by London-based Directors of the Chartered Company, and by echoing the statement, her Majesty appeared to be talking for her Government.

It is admitted that it was not the Imperial Government which planned to invade but the Chartered Company. So why did Queen Victoria repeat a statement by the Company? That question is answered later in this narrative.

The declaration was terse but meaningful, upholding a clause in the petition for a Charter that called for the maintenance of peace and order in Matabeleland at a time when war was still a year away. It was nothing but a recital of lies to deceive Lobengula and the world.

The whole thing was a deception that should not have escaped observation of the granting authority. But the reader must be reminded of the fact that the Pioneer Column had in 1890 occupied Mashonaland without firing a shot.

While members of the Pioneer Column were armed to the teeth to defend the occupation, the local natives made the Column's job easy by welcoming them, believing that they were coming in to defend the "poor Mashona" against the "marauding and ferocious" Matabele forces. An analysis of this poor judgment on the part of the people of Mashonaland will be made later in this narrative.

But it must be noted the Company could not (and would not) in 1893 refer in retrospect to the established fact of its occupation of Mashonaland with no resistance or challenge, to fortify its purported peaceful intentions in both Mashonaland and Matabeleland as claimed in a number of proclamations. Had the people of Mashonaland challenged the occupation, the Pioneer Column would have blasted their way into the territory anyway. In that event the occupation would have lost the Company their only claimed reason, which was that Mashonaland had to be occupied, followed by invasion of Matabeleland, to "protect poor Mashona" against the Matabele. This worked well for the Company because it was left free to mount its propaganda to paint Lobengula black.

It would take until 1897 when white settlers came out in their true colours after the Mashona unwittingly joined the Matabele in rebellion, only for them to be blasted with sticks of dynamite in caves where they had taken refuge. The alleged "protectors" had become executioners of the rebelling Mashona. So much for the Chartered Company's peaceful designs in Mashonaland to "protect" the Mashona! As pressure mounted against Lobengula, a number of things happened, all of which gave the lie to Rhodes' claimed peaceful intentions in Matabeleland. After the Queen's message sent to Lobengula through Moffat, a report in the *Financial News* dated 9 January 1892, a year and nine months before the outbreak of war, read:

"It is a significant fact that at all the forts from Tuli to Salisbury the Chartered Company's flag has been taken down and the Union Jack hoisted in its place. Adding this to the fact that the pioneers have done all in their power to provoke Lobengula, even going so far as to escort Khama's men out of the country, there is no doubt that a fight must ultimately and very shortly follow", read the newspaper."

The Company then held the Royal Charter and no longer cared how that provocative display of defiance would be viewed by the Imperial Government. And there is no known record that the Imperial Government protested the violation of its authority by the Company. What conclusion therefore can be drawn from the Imperial Government's failure to protest such impudent violation of its authority? Was the Imperial Government colluding with the Chartered Company in Matabeleland? Lobengula must have wondered as the clock ticked towards the outbreak of hostilities. The Matabele King was running out of time to prevent invasion, and the British Government was doing nothing to rein in the Chartered Company.

Subsequent to the *Financial News* quoted earlier, Major Forbes announced that plans for the invasion had been completed by 19 July, a month before 14 August 1893 when the secret agreement with mercenaries was signed. Lobengula was increasingly getting concerned, and on 27 July telegraphed to Dr Rutherford Harris in Cape Town:

"I thought you came to dig gold, (a reference to the infamous Rudd Concession and others), but it seems that you have come not only to dig the gold, but to rob me of my people and country as well".

It is significant that Lobengula addressed this complaint to the Imperial Government and not the Chartered Company to whom the concession had been granted. It was clear to the Matabele King that not enough, if anything at all, was being done by the Imperial Government to distance itself away from the Chartered Company.

Therefore, did Lobengula believe that Her Majesty's Government was working with the Company to invade Matabeleland? Did he have any reason to suspect that? Yes, indeed!

On 16 August, two days after the signing of the secret agreement, High Commissioner Sir Henry exchanged bitter words with the king when it was alleged that

Lobengula's forces had fired on Capt. Lendy and his mounted troops while at the same time Sir Henry sarcastically thanked Lobengula for protection he had always extended to white men. This doublespeak must again have left Lobengula wondering on whose side Sir Henry was. There was also the killing of two of Lobengula's peace envoy at Tati on 18 October while there to deliver a peace letter to Sir Henry.

A third member of the envoy and brother of the King went missing without trace. This yet again must have left Lobengula wondering whether British representatives were indeed on his side.

These doubts in the mind of Lobengula arose against the fact that the Matabele Kingdom had treaties of friendship with the United Kingdom. Why did the representatives of the Imperial Government in South Africa treat the subject of treaties with the Matabele with so much disdain or in such cavalier manner? The reader should understand Lobengula was not caught, without provocation, crossing the English Channel to invade the United Kingdom. His kingdom was destroyed because he wanted to be left alone in peace. Lobengula, like his father before him, was unshaken in his resolve to keep white settlers out of his country and was willing to fight to keep the country free of them. He maintained this stance until he was overtaken by events and had to defend himself against formidable odds. But he went to a great deal of trouble trying to work with the British Government, often quoting the 1836 British peace treaty with Mzilikazi. On the other hand, his peace overtures were being blocked by the Chartered Company from reaching Her Majesty's Government, a recipe for disaster for the Matabele which was being created by the Company with the Imperial Government seemingly watching like a disinterested spectator.

It is pertinent that a few examples of his resolve to

avoid war should be recorded for posterity. A Mr Kirby, a resident at Bulawayo, writing to his company, the Tati Concession, said on 18 August:

'From all I hear our Government (the Chartered Company) intend to force Loben (Lobengula) to fight. Most whites I have seen from Bulawayo say that the king does not want to fight.

On 9 September, a Mr. Dawson, an authority on Matabele affairs, wrote to Moffat:

"I am firmly of the opinion that Loben does not want to fight and that he will not do so unless actually forced to do it in self-defence ... The High Commissioner (Sir Henry Loch) has actually sent some very conciliatory messages , and holding the opinion which I do of Loben's intentions, I cannot see where the probability of hostilities occurring becomes apparent, unless, of course, the third factor, i.e the Company, is so powerful as to have its own way in case they wish to see the thing out."

There were several others who spared no effort to rein in Dr. Leander Starr Jameson in endeavours to improve relations with Lobengula.

The attitude of settlers in Mashonaland, however, did not help the situation as shown by a letter by the Imperial Secretary in Cape Town to the Chartered Company on 17 August, 1893, in which he absolved Lobengula of any blame for the deteriorating relations with the Chartered Company, as the situation continued to hurtle at an uncontrollable speed towards an eruption of hostilities.

He wrote: *"The chief, Lobengula, who is apparently anxious for peace, seems to be doing his best to restrain his people, and to protect the lives of the European population which is not unnaturally anxious that an early termination should be put to the present unsettled feeling which prevails, and which they consider can only be attained by the immediate and entire subjugation of the Matabele".*

A point of no return was reached in May 1893 when events finally led to the so-called Victoria Incident which was provoked by the Chartered Company to precipitate war that followed in October. There are conflicting accounts about what led to Mgandane's death with 30 of his men at the hands of Capt. Lendy who was ordered by Leander Starr Jameson to cause an incident as a pretext to provoke war. Reliable information about the incident can be found in John H. Harris's book, *The Chartered Millions* from which a great deal of material in some preceding passages of this book have been drawn.

Harris spared no words to prick the national conscience of the British people, to realize some of the ugliest injustices suffered by the Matabele people at the hands of a bunch of capitalists in their most cruel mission in the name of the so-called civilization.

Harris writes in his book:
"These facts are published with the object, first, of showing how grave has been the injustice to 800 000 native peoples of Southern Rhodesia, and how urgent is the need for such reparation as may still be possible that the public of the British Commonwealth may understand the Rhodesian situation..."

Harris wrote this in 1920 when the book was published. He may have been writing in 2019 when reparations have become an urgent call among the people of Matabeleland. Useful material used in this book has also been gleaned from Peter Baxter's book *Rhodesia, Last Outpost of the British Empire 1890 – 1980*.

This book, though written with the idea of glorifying the occupation of what became Southern Rhodesia, provides some balancing historical account on the tragic

Victoria Incident. Substantial material has also been drawn from accounts of the 1893 war as recorded in the book, *The Downfall of Lobengula* by W. A. Willis and L. T. Collingridge, with contributions from Maj. P. W. Forbes, Maj. Sir John C. Willoughby, Mr. IL Rider Haggard, Mr. F. C Selous and Mr. P. B. S. Ivrey.

The Victoria Incident is of profound interest, especially to the Matabele people who suffered most cruelly as a result of it, while at the same time being blamed by the establishment for allegedly provoking the tragedy.

It is noteworthy that the Chartered Company was spoiling to provoke war and was to sign a secret agreement with white settlers to precipitate it. It is important, therefore, that no time or space should be spared to give a fair account of the incident and what led to it.

It was a trivial matter of stolen telegraph wire, stolen cattle, and a disputed border that finally triggered the war, with horrendous results for the Matabele. It is imperative to record at this stage the fact that Lobengula only grudgingly accepted the Jameson Line of June 1891 as a boundary between his territory and the British Protectorate of Mashonaland. This explains why Mgandane and Manyewu denied any knowledge of the border when confronted by Jameson and told to move on and cross the border or else the impulsive Jameson would send his troopers to drive them across the border. It was during that mission, a couple of hours later, that Mgandane and his warriors were overtaken, and he was gunned down and killed with 30 of his men, without, as it will be shown, any provocation.

He had carried a letter from Lobengula to Jameson warning him that he was sending warriors to recover stolen cattle and "punish the Amaswina" for the missing cattle and for their "cutting of the white man's telegraph wire" for which three chiefs were being accused.

Lobengula acted with great restraint to avoid a breakdown of the already strained relations with white settlers at Fort Victoria, among whose cattle Lobengula's missing cattle were found.

In Ndebele culture, stealing a king's cattle was an overt act of declaring war. The world should be reminded that it was the subject of cattle that forced a rupture between Tshaka and Mzilikazi, forcing the latter to flee from Zululand. Early in May 1893, reports were rife in Fort Victoria that someone had cut and carried away 500 meters of the Company's telegraph wire, with allegations that chief Gomalla was the culprit. The Company's local agents levied a fine of a considerable number of cattle that turned out to belong to Lobengula which chief Gomalla kept for the king. The chief Gomalla quickly paid the fine with Lobengula's cattle! This was a capital crime in Ndebele society. The Company claimed the cattle were returned to Gomalla, although no reason was given for this gesture when cutting 500 metres of telegraph line disrupted communication with the outside world, and the cost of restoring it was considerable. Lobengula denied the claim that the cattle in question had been returned.

Writing to Moffat on 10 May 1893, Colenbrander says the Company y seized the cattle as punishment for the alleged wire-cutting, not for the lie proclaimed by the Chartered Company that Lobengula's warriors had attacked white men near Fort Victoria!

"...*Company seized all their cattle, which turn(ed) out to be the king's. Loben (Lobengula) is awfully wild about this. The people wanted permission to recapture them, which fortunately was refused them, or otherwise what would have been the result? I have written to Drs (Rutherford) Harris and (Leander Starr) Jameson to be more careful in their seizures, as these matters may not always be taken by the king so coolly".*

But what manner of the law of the jungle was being applied here by white British subjects? These men were not by any standard honourable. They were libertines in the loose to rampage, brigands who knew no law out there "to teach the Matabele a lesson of their life". They were spoiling for a fight with Lobengula at the slightest pretext, while provoking the king to wage war. They were liars who used this tactic to precipitate war for which they had acquired an assortment of weapons of precision against natives wielding primitive weapons.

They had five units of the devastating Maxim gun and artillery with which to shell Matabele positions to prevent close combat. They then went home puffed with pride! Lobengula, on the other hand, was determined to avoid war but was being frustrated when he tried to draw the attention of the Imperial Government to the threat posed by the Chartered Company.

Before looking at how the wire cutting was viewed by white settlers at Fort Victoria, let us look at a report by Captain Norris Newman, Reuter Special Correspondent based in the township. His report aptly sums up the local situation at the time.

Later we will look at the mood of white settlers and how they viewed the wire cutting. Newman writes:

"At last matters were brought to a head by some of the marauders cutting down the telegraph poles, for which they were promptly brought to book and ordered to pay a fine, which was paid by the petty chiefs, Setama and Gomalla, apparently out of the cattle held by them in charge for the king. Communications passed between the Administrator and Lobengula, and later on with the High Commissioner (Sir Henry) in which the king denied that it was his people who had done the damage and objected to the fine being levied. He then sent an impi in July 1893, under the Induna Umgandane, ostensibly to punish the

people who had cut the telegraph wires, but these men, whether they mistook or exceeded their orders, tackled some friendly Mashonas, killed some, and chased others right into Fort Victoria, where the poor unfortunates tried to take refuge. The officially acknowledged number of those who were killed did not exceed seven, against 400 alleged by Capt. Paul Forbes and others.

The following explains Lobengula's view of the wire-cattle-boundary question to which I referred earlier:

This message was sent to John Moffat, the British Assistant Commissioner at Palapye, and must be reproduced in full to enable the reader a balanced picture of what was really going on amid mounting pressures and vicious propaganda, which were being brought to bear on Lobengula's life.

"*I have received your wire (in which) you accuse me wrongfully. I only sent my impi to recover some of my stolen cattle and to punish the Amaswina that your people complained to me about as constantly cutting your telegraph wires, but it would seem now to me that the white people stole my cattle, for white people know very well that the Amaswina had stolen some of my cattle, for I had written to tell Dr. Jameson, so what have you got to say now?*

"*You said before that you would not punish my Amahole (vassals), but now that I send my impis to punish them for you for harm done to your telegraph wire you resent it –what goods have my impi stolen and destroyed, and how many cattle have they captured?*

"*I am not aware of any boundary between Dr. Jameson and myself. Who gave him the boundary? Let him come forward and show me the man that pointed out to him these boundaries; I know nothing whatever about them, and you Moffat, you know very well that the white people have done this thing on purpose.*

This is not right. My people only came to punish the Amahole for stealing my cattle and cutting your wires."

The accusation was, of course, found to be without good cause, but no apology was forthcoming from Lobengula's accusers. The attitude was that the perfidious Matabele King did not deserve an apology. But before going further, let me clarify the confusion arising from the existence or not of the Jameson Line which became the official border between Matabeleland and Mashonaland. In 2016, writing in a local daily, a correspondent pointed out that Lobengula had denied the existence of the Jameson Line. How could I assert there was indeed the Jameson Line?

The Jameson Line, as the name implies, was a creation of the Administrator of the Chartered Company, Dr. Leander Starr Jameson. It was not a subject of negotiation and agreement between Lobengula and Jameson. Jameson enforced the boundary and maps were drawn showing its route. When in July 1893 Jameson ordered Mgandane and his forces to retreat beyond the border, they simply pleaded ignorance about it because it was unknown to them until then. It is important to mention the fact that the maps showing the route were drawn by the Chartered Company. This accorded with the Berlin Conference resolution of 1859 pertaining to international boundaries.

Before looking at other sources of 'facts' on which the Company relied to explain away the Victoria Incident, which due to being repeated over and over again as fact, had a damaging effect on Lobengula's image and character, let us look at other independent sources of information.

CHAPTER 4

THE VICTORIA INCIDENT

WRITING in his book, *Rhodesia, Last Outpost of the British Empire 1890 – 1980,* Peter Baxter says, with the establishment of white settlers in Fort Victoria, the telegraph nosed its way north through Mashonaland, all manner of theft became commonplace among local natives. "What liberties the Mashona clans were emboldened to take with the Matabele they took no less with the settlers. The lifting of miles of copper wire became routine. "On a few occasions Jameson himself dealt only slightly less heavily with miscreant Mashona chiefs than did the Matabele".

He goes on to explain that copper wire thefts were costly and disrupted communication with the world at large. This, it will be noted, is another way of saying the lives of white settlers depended on the maintenance of the telegraph lines in a working order. Thefts of wire were, therefore, a matter of life or death as it turned out, for both the miscreant Mashona and potentially, the settlers.

"At the core of much of the tension between the Matabele and the Company's administration was the tendency among the Mashona to enact mischief which annoyed both Europeans and Matabele", Baxter writes.

He volunteers an admission, however, that in the case of the theft of copper wire from the vital telegraph installations the theft "was more than just an annoyance". Thefts destroyed communications and cost the Company a great deal of money. This, one can conclude, forced Jameson to deal with the Mashona in a manner earlier described.

"In order for it to be clearly understood that the practice must cease, fines and other repercussions were harsh". The use of the word "harsh" is an understatement of the gravity of the matter. The use of the word "deadly" would have been more appropriate. Baxter reveals that in one particular case "a heavy fine in cattle to be paid with beasts that in fact belonged to the Matabele" was levied.

There is a well-known case in which a chief refused to surrender the cattle.

Capt. Lendy galloped back to camp to summon reinforcements. The group went back to the chief's village and massacred the chief and 30 of his people. This massacre was blamed on the Matabele and the number of dead inflated from 30 to 400. Before further incidents designed to make Lobengula blameworthy, comment must be made about how white men value human life to the value of 500 metres of copper wire.

Without in anyway seeking to deny that a length of copper wire was probably stolen, but what is the proportional value of human life to that length of telegraph wire? Can the blood of 30 souls that perished with their chief be a propitiation for 500 metres of copper wire, even in the most rabid capitalist system? In his quest to defend wrong-doing on the part of the Chartered Company, Baxter in the following passage paints a horrifying picture of the manner the Matabele allegedly conducted themselves during the raid to "punish the Amaswina", ignoring the undisputed fact that the warriors were under strict orders to behave themselves, especially concerning the white settlers.

Lobengula told British authorities, Sir Henry Loch to be precise, that his warriors had been disarmed before entering camp in Fort Victoria, to deliver a letter explaining their mission. But in the interest of a balanced examination of what happened, Baxter must be allowed to give his side of the story in the wake of the raid.

- " . . . then Lobengula unexpectedly deployed north a more aggressive force than had hitherto been seen. His intention was not only to deal with the errant parties but also set a general example to all the Mashona in the territory, with the additional object of making it known to the whites that the Mashona still laid within his jurisdiction. This was a highly provocative ploy and suggested difficult internal pressures. Probably hoping that Jameson would accept the raid for what it was, Lobengula put his men under fear of death regarding any aggressive action against the whites".

- "In the beginning, Jameson did take the action for what it was, but some loosening of the king's authority was evident in local commanders exceeding this very restricted rule of engagement. As the raid gathered momentum Jameson was forced to think again".

- 'The Matabele fell on the tribes in the vicinity of Fort Victoria with shocking ferocity. Whites were appalled at the degree of violence applied, with wanton and apparently senseless torture of men, women and children".

The whites whose mission was the protection of the Mashona watched as mere spectators while this alleged massacre of the Mashona proceeded!

The first notable omission in this account is the number of those who were killed. It is also common knowledge that the raid during which, it has been proved, no more than seven people, all of them men were killed. It is also true that the raid took place a week before Jameson arrived in Fort Victoria from his base in Salisbury. Furthermore, the world is not told by Baxter why whites allowed this to happen under their very noses, when their mission in Mashonaland was the protection of the "poor Mashona" against the Matabele. They were well armed to contain the situation provoked by 300 Matabele armed with spears.

And they did not even take their weapons into the fort because they were disarmed before going in. How did they commit all the crimes attributed to them with Lendy and his troopers watching with folded arms? When Capt Lendy was ordered by Jameson to follow the Matabele forces and drive them across the "border", he had 38 heavily armed men with him. Where was Lendy and his men when the carnage reported with so much relish took place?

In the following report of a commission of inquiry, the fore-going claims will be discredited and shown to be part of a ploy to justify invasion of Matabeleland.

Sir F. J. Newton was appointed by the Imperial authorities to investigate the circumstances of the Victoria Incident. According to his report, the Matabele warriors arrived in Victoria district on 9 July 1893. Their object was to punish the Mashona for stealing Lobengula's cattle and cutting Sir Starr Jameson's telegraph wire. For a week before Sir Starr Jameson arrived, they bullied the Mashona, killing men and women, before taking away a number of girls. Sir Jameson arrived and had a pally with Chief Mgandane and Manyewu. He then ordered them across the border, giving them a couple of hours before he sent Capt. Lendy to lead 38 mounted troopers to drive them across the border. They were found before crossing the border, which they did not know, and Lendy gunned down Mgandane and 30 others. It was for all intents and purposes a massacre.

Although the company accused them of opening fire on Lendy and his men, Sir Newton's report says, "there was nothing to show that any organized or individual resistance was offered". The number of Mgandane's impis ranged between 500 and 800 men, against 8 000 claimed by the Company. A questionable feature of this report is its failure to say where Capt. Lendy and his 38 mounted troopers were when the alleged massacre of 400 men, women and children near Fort Victoria happened

It was later established that the alleged "ferocity" was in fact a gross exaggeration out of all proportion with reality. Frederick Selous makes the amazing statement concerning the Mashona who were allegedly killed during the raid.

He said:

"It is true that no white man was murdered by the Matabele during the prosecution of this historical raid, but, short of this, everything was done to stir up the bitterest feelings of exasperation in the hearts of the colonists. By "everything" Selous is referring to the protection of the Mashona for whose purpose, it has been repeated many times, the Pioneer Column allegedly occupied Mashonaland. What happened to the will to defend the "poor Mashona" when all this happened?

More than 400 Mashona men, women and children were, according to Capt. Forbes, killed in the neighbourhood of the township of Victoria'. Subsequent information was to show that Forbes' statement to Selous was grossly and cruelly inaccurate.

The following is Jameson's own account:

'The indunas arrived after my last telegram; after some conversations, during which they would not consent to

return beyond the border, I told them I would give them an hour to retire, and if they did not, would send my men to drive them out as I had informed the king.

"At the stated time Captain Lendy, and thirty-eight mounted men, rod out, found about 300 still on commonage; these fired on Lendy's party. Lendy then fired, and pursued (them) for about nine miles, a few men were killed, including two head men. Lendy returned; no casualties".

And this is the same Lendy who did not raise a finger to protect the Mashona when they were chased into Fort Victoria where they sought protection.

Mgandane was one of the two head men killed, but there is still no conclusive information about Manyewu's fate, although it seems he was among those killed with Mgandane. Manyewu was Lobengula's trusted envoy sent with the letter to pacify Jameson. Although questions were asked about the border and Imperial authorities were unable to shed light on the subject at this point, the border was Jameson's creation, enforced with arms of war that Lobengula did not have.

The Victoria Incident marked the beginning of what became known as the Jameson Line. But it was not until June 1891 that it became known and Mashonaland was proclaimed a British Protectorate by an Order in Council of the British Parliament.

But the first time Lobengula's impis heard about it was when Jameson talked about it before Mgandane and Manyewu. It will be shown that Lobengula knew nothing about it until those sent to Victoria with Mgandane reported its existence.

But Selous' figure of 400 Mashona killed during the raid to punish those who were accused of stealing cattle and some telegraph wire, was shown to be an exaggeration so gross as to be well-nigh criminal, according to John Harris. In Mr. Newton's report none of the evidence supported Mr. Selous' allegations. Several witnesses, however, saw between two and seven killed. Jameson himself said "altogether about twenty were killed in Victoria".

The raid took place a week before his arrival, but is the suggestion that there was no one in Fort Victoria that week with authority to order Lendy and his men to protect the Mashona? If 8 000 impis, as claimed by Forbes, had actually come to attack the settlers would they wait for Jameson to order them to defend themselves and the Mashona?

A year earlier, Captain Lendy was involved in a punitive expedition against the Mashona for which he was berated and condemned for using excessive violence. These were the very same people for whose protection was proclaimed to the world as the reason for the occupation of Mashonaland, and the subsequent invasion of Matabeleland.

It is pertinent that mention must be made of the fact that Rhodes pronounced in November 1893 the kingdom as a principality, followed in December 1894 by the Orders - in - Council that p proclaimed the territory Matabeleland.

The Capt. Lendy incident, therefore, became a foretaste of what was to come. But poor learners though they proved themselves to be, nearly seven hundred Mashona allowed themselves to be recruited as batmen when the settlers invaded Matabeleland in 1893. As it will be shown in following pages of this book, the Victoria Incident marked the beginning of a British-Mashona marriage of convenience that years later was to lead to a white-black coalition against the Matabele. That consequently led to the commission of genocide against the Matabele.

This genocidal coalition is detailed in my book *The*

Rule by Conquest the Struggle in Mthwakazi of which this book is a more detailed historical successor. As revealed in the first book, the people of Matabeleland have suffered two genocides at the hands of the Mashona working with the British in the last century. A year before the Victoria Incident, Capt. Lendy was involved in a punitive expedition against the Mashona. The expedition came about as a result of a complaint by a white farmer that he had been robbed by one chief Ngomo.

Lendy was sent out by Sir Starr Jameson to arrest the chief and bring him to book. Ngomo, displaying unusual courage against such heavy odds, refused to be arrested, and Lendy galloped back to camp for more mounted troopers, armed with rifles, a seven- pounder and a Maxim machine gun to kill Ngomo and 21 of his people. The arsenal of arms of war used gives the impression that Sir Starr Jameson had decided to declare war against the entire population of Victoria Province, and not a man and 20 odd of his people armed, if at all, with sticks.

If one is looking for evidence that the policy of the Chartered Company was to exterminate the natives, the Lendy Incident is among such evidence.

Writing to Dr. Rutherford Harris months before the outbreak of the war in 1893, King Lobengula put it aptly:

"I thought you came to dig gold, but it seems that you have come not only to dig the gold, but to rob me of my people and country as well".

Those detractors of Lobengula who continue to accuse him of selling his country to the whites for a bowl of sugar might pluck up courage to apologize.

This is how Capt. Lendy described his expedition to bring Ngomo to book:

"I counted twenty-one killed, among them being the chief Gomo himself. I captured forty-seven head of cattle and several goats. Deeming the punishment sufficient I did not burn the huts, and I left what little grain there was".

These cattle belonged to Lobengula.

One might be excused the question: what good were the huts or "the little grain there was" when its owners lay dead? Were there any children in the kraal who watched as their parents were butchered in cold blood or is it that the children were also killed?

Lendy did not have the moral courage to volunteer the information and admit that the children watched as 23 members of the community were gunned down for trying to protect their property.

But the Lendy episode cannot be allowed to pass without further comment. It is clear, and an undisputed fact, that Lendy's so-called punishment far exceeded that allegedly inflicted upon the Mashona by the Matabele which followed Lendy's expedition only a year later. History has recorded "that the punishment inflicted in this case, involving the loss of some twenty-three lives, appears utterly disproportionate to the original offence."

These are words of Mr. Newton who was appointed to investigate the Victoria Incident when the Company frantically tried to cover up wrongdoing by its servants while it continued to churn out propaganda aimed at condemning the "perfidious Matabele" as the sole criminals. But a question that begs to be asked is: was perfidy the only crime or the Matabele the only offenders on the ground? Lord Knutsford provides the answer in the following report on the Lendy expedition:

"The full report by Capt. Lendy, subsequently received and forwarded, would, in Lord Knutsford's opinion, have justified much stronger terms of condemnation than were used by the High Commissioner.

"There is nothing in the information now before his Lordship which affords any justification of Capt. Lendy's proceedings, and after making for the difficulties attending the establishment of a European administration in a country like Mashonaland, Lord Knutsford cannot avoid the conclusion that Capt. Lendy acted in this matter with recklessness and undue harshness". Strong words indeed!

But what indeed were "the difficulties attending the establishment of a European administration in a country like Mashonaland" when history has recorded that the colonist occupied that territory without firing a shot because the Mashona welcomed the colonist, and later joined them in the invasion of Matabeleland?

The English language is rich with its idiosyncrasies and so Lord Knutsford was perfectly right to use the word "recklessness" where justice would have been served better by using the word "criminal" instead. The world must heed that the Company at this point in time was not at war with the natives of Victoria who were supposed to be under its protection. The Chartered Company, however, pretended that they were providing that protection, and that the Matabele were not making it easy for them to accomplish their noble mission. This was a campaign to vilify and slander Lobengula.

So how could Sir Leander Starr Jameson sanction the use of heavy weapons of war that Capt. Lendy and company took to the scene where they left 23 villagers dead, if this was not to show the world that the settlers would not stop rushing into where angels feared to tread?

Jameson was a man puffed up with the sin of impulsive callousness, aggressive intent and self-aggrandizement as was to be shown when he led an unprovoked aggressive raid into neighbouring South African Republic in 1896 where he finally met his Waterloo.

But since he had no match in Victoria and the territory

of Matabeleland where he was about to launch another unprovoked military expedition, what was better for him to occupy his evil designs against the natives than sending his notorious messenger to massacre unarmed Mashona? Since it is a matter of profound interest to the people of Matabeleland in particular, and indeed the world, the Victoria Incident offers a unique opportunity to examine all possible avenues to expose Jameson's evil designs to mislead the world as he prepared to wage war against the people of Matabeleland.

John H. Harris' book already mentioned provides an unparalleled source of information on the incident.

"One of the most material features of the Victoria Incident arose from Sir Starr Jameson's allegation that when Capt. Lendy caught up with the Matabele as they slowly marched toward that elusive "border" which was the subject of so much controversy, the Matabele fired on Lendy and his men. It has been established that they did nothing of the sort".

But this episode in the series of provocative actions to precipitate war had serious repercussion for Lobengula. Reproduced below is the record of Sir Starr Jameson's report.

"And people rode out, found about 300 (Matabele) still on commonage; these fired on Lendy's party".

This report was dispatched to the High Commissioner, Sir Henry Loch on 18 July 1893. Lobengula was running out of time, with the outbreak of war only two months away. Two days later, Sir Henry telegraphed Lobengula vigorously arguing with the king about the incident.

"Dr. Jameson made friendly endeavours to restrain your people and induce them to retire, but when the conduct of your indunas and people became dangerous not only to the property but to the lives of the white men, and they dared to fire on white men, then the limits of patience were passed". This was a servant of the Imperial Government defending Jameson. This allegation against Lobengula and his warriors was later proved officially to be wholly unfounded. An interesting feature of this incident can be found in Sir F. Newton's findings and reaction:

Dr. Jameson was misinformed when he reported officially that the Matabele fired first on the whites . . . the sergeant of the advance guard (Lendy) fired the first shot, the Matabele practically offered no resistance".
The Matabele practically offered no resistance means that they did not fire on Lendy or provoke him to fire on them.

This was the conclusion of a man, though still a civil servant of the Imperial Government at this time was to become an employee of the Chartered Company. Those who knew the truth about this incident were being bought off to protect the image of the Company! Neither the Company nor Sir Starr Jameson offered an apology regarding the gross loss of life, and injustice caused the Matabele people. Jameson's attitude was that the Matabele deserved no apology. These are the standards of behaviour that the white man exported to the African continent to be accepted as an element of the so-called civilization. The developments in Victoria were being watched in London with great interest, and on 25 July, Lord Ripon drew the attention of the Chartered Company to the developments in Fort Victoria.
This chapter of the Victoria Incident cannot be closed without looking at what was happening around Lobengula. There had been more unfounded allegations

against the Matabele to the effect that kraals of friendly natives in Mashonaland were being burnt down. In a number of cases, the alleged kraals did not even exist. And where was Capt. Lendy when all this was supposed to be happening?

A local newspaper *The Times* quoted Dr. Jameson as telling a committee of Fort Victoria settlers that "everything was ready to push affairs to an issue", alluding to the invasion of Matabeleland.

The Victoria Agreement was about to be signed on 14 August, only two months before the invasion of Lobengula's country. There was, however, no let up on pressure build-up for the king's discomfort. On 16 August, only two days after the secret agreement, the High Commissioner ordered his assistant J. Moffat to tell Lobengula that Sir Henry was still for peace, as if Lobengula was the aggressor against England!

But the High Commissioner was adamant peace lay with Lobengula, and Sir Henry said: "I have no intention of invading his country or dragging him into war; that although the white man is fully prepared to fight if he forces them to do so, peace or war will rest with him".

This is the first known official statement of fact that the Imperial Government, while pretending to be against invasion of Matabeleland, actually sanctioned the invasion.

No one should be fooled by Sir Henry's doublespeak, the message to Lobengula was patently clear: play ball or else! Lobengula was being told to open the floodgates into his country or face the music. How could peace rest with him when no hair of a white man had been harmed for as long as human memory could recall?

But in the last few months before the out-break of war, Lobengula had suffered cruelly at the hands of the white man, losing a leading member of his establishment in the ill- fated Victoria Raid and, as if this incident was not enough, two peace envoys waiting to deliver Lobengula's peace message to Sir Henry, were murdered outside his office with a third member of the three-man envoy and member of his household escaping instant death, but disappearing without trace, all this in circumstance that can only be described as suspect. The envoys apparently were victims of a lynching gang to prevent the message reaching the Imperial authorities at Palapye. (The reader should note that induna Mgandane, veteran of many battles, was a brother of Queen Lozikeyi, one of Lobengula's wives, while Manyewu was a trusted commander of one of the king's regiments).

The Imperial Government at one stage appeared to be increasingly becoming concerned about the Chartered Company's intransigence while Lobengula, under mounting pressure, became frantic in his peace bid to avert war which he was sure he could not win.

The following message from the Imperial Secretary to the Company dated 17 August 1893, just three days after the signing of the Victoria Secret Agreement to wage war with the king, reveals the level of a growing concern in high places while those concerned futilely tried to avert a catastrophe.

"To enable Lobengula to have a fair chance of arriving at a peaceable settlement of existing difficulties, his Excellency desires to see excitement allayed and confidence restored, but his efforts in that direction will be to a great extent neutralized by the publication of sensational Press telegrams, such as those which have recently appeared. His Excellency desires me, therefore, to invite your co-operation by your giving instructions to the officers of the British South Africa Company to exercise prudence and moderation in their communications with the representatives of the Press". This was three days after the signing of the secret agreement that committed the Chartered Company to invade Matabeleland. An unavoidable question is: Were the Imperial Government authorities unaware of plans and moves to invade Matabeleland? It would be difficult for most people who knew how closely officers of the Imperial Government had been working with the Company, to enable them to secure the Moffat Treaty and, in due course, the granting of the Royal Charter, not to believe that they knew about the Company's plans but pretended that the key to peace lay with Lobengula. This means that the threatening breach of peace could be avoided by opening the floodgates for the occupation of the kingdom.

It was a conspiracy involving the Company and officials of the Imperial Government that went tragically wrong for the people of Matabeleland. Only on 16 August 1893 the High Commissioner had written to Moffat saying, quote: "…that although the white man is fully prepared to fight if he forces (by refusing to open the flood gates) them to do so …" He added that war or peace would depend on Lobengula! When the High Commissioner was a frontline witness of Lobengula's frantic efforts to avert war but had no Press agents to counteract vicious Company propaganda to justify invasion and war?

CHAPTER 5

THE FATAL DAY

The fatal day for the people of Matabeleland was the signing in Fort Victoria on 14 August 1893 of the secret Agreement to invade the Kingdom. For months prior to the signing of the agreement white settlers in both Fort Victoria and Salisbury had been agitating and calling for action, threatening to pull out of the territory of Mashonaland they had now been occupying for four years. It was, of course, a bluff to get Jameson to act.

Leaders of the agitating settlers were accused by Leander Starr Jameson of being "fair weather" knee-shaking cowards and were told in no uncertain terms that no one would miss them if they carried out their threats and left the country. There are no known records that there were any who decided to pull out of the pending expedition at this crucial moment, with the Secret Agreement offering them incentives of a lifetime about to be signed.

Studies of colonial history in India, Nigeria and Uganda, to name just a few, show that the rights of local natives were always upheld, respecting customary laws and practices.

In these countries the king or local chief held the land in trust for the people, with adequate provisions to prevent the king or chief alienating land rights without the approval of the local chief's council. The position was the same under the Matabele monarchy. The land rights and practices cannot be assailed by legislation or constitutional laws. They are entrenched by tradition and customary law. Anyone who assails land rights of natives can, if possible, take away the air they breathe and the water that sustains their life. The Chartered Company stopped short of taking away air and water from the people of Matabeleland because this was not possible for them to do.

Readers will note that in Zimbabwe hegemony has been used by the ruling black apartheid regime, otherwise known as the Axis of Tribalism, to over-ride customary law and practice as a political instrument to occupy Matabeleland, while denying the Matabele rights to occupy land in Mashonaland. This was not sanctioned by any legislation or provision in the constitution. It is a political strategy in which the policy is enforced by civil servants all of whom are drawn from tribes in the ruling axis of tribalism, under the watchful eye of security forces, in case the victims offered resistance.

This ensures that even provisions of the constitution, like devolution of power, that would work for the participation of local personnel, are negated by the administration which is packed with appointees whose only qualification is their tribe. This ensures that local people are effectively denied employment in their own land!

For the people of Matabeleland, there is, therefore, no room for redressing their grievances. In the land ambit, for instance, local chiefs were not involved in the redistribution programme to ensure that their people benefitted. The result is that Matabeleland has been packed with millions of people from Mashonaland where not a single foot of a Matabele is allowed to tread. The Matabele have since the land reform of 2000 been squeezed out of space and forced to be happy with their rulers. A number of Matabele who unwittingly bought farms in Mashonaland before 2000 soon discovered that they were not safe to remain there.

One ugly case of a man who had bought a farm long before the inception of the land programme was one day, soon after the launch of the reform programme, beaten up by his own employees and left for dead, years after he had been farming in the Headlands, area east of Harare.

I must address an appeal, first, to SADC, the peacemaker in the region, secondly, the African Union, the continental body responsible in the realm of peace in Africa. These two bodies have for far too long given the ZANU PF regime in Zimbabwe a free rein to violently oppress the people of Matabeleland. Indeed, my appeal must also go to the United Nations whose rules of engagement with the oppressed people of the world have since inception of the world body in 1945, become too antiquated and archaic to serve those in Africa who are still carrying the burden of oppression. The people of Matabeleland are extremely dismayed to note that countries like South Africa are talking about pulling out of the International Criminal Court of Justice because of alleged claims that the ICCJ is targeting African leaders. The pull out will be tantamount to giving license to totalitarian regimes in Africa which in turn would intensify the oppression of their own people.

The people of Matabeleland as a tribe are being targeted for rule with an iron rod and unprecedented tyranny. Why has South Africa, of all countries, chosen to lead the exodus from the voluntary body when the oppressed people of Matabeleland are looking to the republic for moral support against first the Mugabe and now the Mnangagwa regime?

CHAPTER 6

THE SECRET AGREEMENT

THE agreement was drafted in Harare and signed by Jameson and addressed to Capt. Alan Wilson in Fort Victoria. Capt. Wilson is the man who was destined to perish with 33 comrades on the banks of the Shangani River, hardly four months later.

It starts by saluting him.

The following are the conditions of service for the members of the Victoria Force for Matabeleland:

1. That each member shall have protection on all claims in Mashonaland until six months after the date of cessation of hostilities.

2. That each member shall be entitled to mark out a farm of three thousand morgen (6, 000 acres) in any part of Matabeleland. No occupation is required, but a quitrent will be charged on each farm of ten shillings per annum.

3. That no marking out of farms and claims will be allowed or held valid until such time as the Administrator and the different columns consider the country sufficiently peaceful, and a week's clear notification will be given to that effect.

4. That members be allowed four clear months wherein to mark out and register their farms, and that no such marking out or registration will be valid after that time with the exception of the rights belonging to Members of the force killed, invalided or dying in service.

5. The Government retain the right at any time

to purchase farms from the Members at the rate of three pounds sterling per morgen and compensation for all improvements. This does not include the purchase of claims already pegged out on farms.

6. That any member of the Victoria Force is entitled to 15 claims on reef and 5 on alluvial claims. The Protection works to be: thirty feet shaft within six months, or sixty feet shaft within twelve months on reef claims. Alluvial claims are to be subject to existing laws in Mashonaland.

7. The "loot" shall be divided one-half to the B.S.A Company and the remainder to the officers and men in equal shares.

8. Each man to be mounted and equipped and rationed when practicable.

9. For the protection of members of the Pioneer Force, no marking out of claims will be allowed on the part of fresh arrivals until four months have elapsed from the time specified in Clause 4

10. From that date on which the Force crosses the border, the rights of any Member of the Force dying, invalided or killed on service shall be protected and secured to his estate. The agreement bears the signature of Leander Starr Jameson for the Chartered Company.

11. This supplementary clause states that in the event of payable gold being discovered upon any farm, no mining or milling for a profit or floatation can take place until the farmers' rights are satisfied according to clause 5, which gives the Company first option to purchase the property on which such payable gold claim has been discovered.

The Company was taking no chances to let such claims slip out its control for the control of the farmer. Under clause 10, members of the invading force became owners of a total of

21 million acres upon crossing the border into Matabeleland!

If there was at this point still any lingering doubt that the Company was determined to wage war after at least four years of preparation, the signing of the secret agreement marked the climax of such preparations to advance the Chartered Company's greed and avarice to expropriate native land rights for the Company's commercial gain.

No human effort could reverse the moves to save the people from the ravages of an un- folding tragedy of catastrophic proportions for the people of Matabeleland.

A cruel irony of the Company's move was that the world would remain ignorant of the secret agreement for many years to come - not that knowing about it before the war actually broke out would have prevented it or made any difference for 77 years. The world remains largely ignorant of the existence of the agreement.

Now a point has been reached to examine the far-reaching implications of the Secret Agreement that led the British South Africa Company to launch a heinous military expedition, not only to rob the people of Matabeleland of their land, steal an un- determinable number of their cattle, but also to commit genocide of horrendous proportions using precision weapons of war totally out of proportion to the primitive weapons with which the people of Matabeleland defended themselves. That Lobengula's forces still managed to account for a good number of invading forces when so formidable amour was arrayed against them, was no small feat.

The invading forces' excuse was to advance the "the dawn of civilization" by shedding the blood of natives in a war whose shocking results were predetermined before the final body was counted and the material gain by the invaders was determined when they crossed the border into Matabeleland.

John Harris' book *The Chartered Millions* says the destruction of the kingdom by the British South Africa Company was without precedent in the world.

At this moment no argument is advanced upon the ethics of this (secret agreement) inducement; of that the reader must be judge; but it will at once be apparent that a complete expropriation of the Matabele was a foregone conclusion, and that this document rendered hopeless the efforts of the Imperial authorities and Lobengula to prevent the invasion of Matabeleland.

There is but one reflection which may perhaps be permitted upon this agreement. It surely could not have been known, at least one hopes not, to the London Directors and the shareholders of the Chartered Company; indeed, it is probable that its publication at the insistence of Mr. Leslie Scott (the man who represented the people of Matabeleland in the land Conference of 1919) in the Appendices of Documents for the Judicial Committee of the Privy Council was the first knowledge most of them had of the existence of such an amazing document.

But this secret agreement does not stand alone; Sir Starr Jameson was not the only person who, whilst his Directors were giving public and official assurances of peaceful intentions, were preparing behind the scenes to act like other 'publicans and sinners' whose wicked example they were so loudly and publicly (as it were) thanking God they did not intend to follow.

The unofficial story issued by those who took a leading part in "smashing" the Matabele is extraordinarily instructive – it is not now and has not been for years procurable in Great Britain. The story was published in a book entitled *The Downfall of Lobengula,* written with the admitted assistance of the principal local officials of the Company Harris quotes the following disclosures from the book:

"Later on, on 13 July of the same year (1889), a petition was presented praying for a Charter".

This resulted in the granting of the latter on 29 October 1889, on which date also this bold enterprise was incorporated as a *joint-stock* concern (not many of us ordinary mortals know what a joint stock concern is) with a capital of a million shares sterling.

So far all had gone smoothly. But now the formidable task of effective occupation – to use the Foreign Office term – had to be faced.

It was universally believed at the time that the Matabele could not be trusted to fulfil their bargain, and recognized authorities expressed the opinion that it would be impossible to enter into possession of Mashonaland without a force of at least 5 000 men.

This opinion, however, was not shared by Mr. Frank Johnson, who afterwards became a Major in the British South Africa Company's military service.

He knew the country well and had acquired a reputation for exceptional daring and resource. His view was that 500 men would be ample for the purpose; and on being invited to do so, tendered to carry the military occupation for 90 000 pounds sterling. This extremely novel offer was accepted, and Major Johnson immediately set about the formation of the historic Mashonaland Pioneers, a *corps d'lite* of Englishmen and colonists, all expert short, and horsemen, of all trades and professions, and numbering 192 men.

It should be noted, however, that when the Company submitted its petition for a Charter, one of its clauses proposed the maintenance of 'peace and order' in Matabeleland".

How could the Company accuse the Matabele of

perfidy while behind the scenes they were working overtime to frustrate peace overtures by Lobengula for which the king was rewarded, in one shocking incident, with the murder of two envoys about to deliver a peace message to Sir Henry Loch, while a third member and brother to Lobengula, disappeared in what, it appears, members of the Bechuanaland Border Police were the only party armed with firearms?

How could the Matabele "keep their side of the bargain" when their peace messages were being intercepted and not allowed to reach the Imperial authorities and be affected?

For the princely sum of ninety thousand pounds sterling the Company secured the services of Frank Johnson to invade Matabeleland, fulfilling the Company's much-vaunted mission to protect "poor Mashona" against the "perfidious and ferocious" Matabele. But the world knows now that the promised "protection" was but a pretext to justify the invasion of Matabeleland.

The world also knows that the so-called protectors were to become the executioners of the Mashona when they displayed such foolishness as to join the Matabele in 1896 in an uprising against their much-acclaimed protectors?

The company's answer to the Mashona rebellion was to send its troops to flush them out by lobbing sticks of dynamite into the caves where the people had taken refuge. That was the "dawn of civilization" promised the world so loudly at the launch of the campaign to subjugate the Matabele. There are features of the secret agreement that are novel and will probably remain so for all time in the history of the British Empire. One feature of the agreement that stands out like a sore thumb is the provision that nowhere limits the operation of the invading force to a "protection" of Mashonaland. But perhaps it is the provision to confiscate and alienate in advance 4 000 000 acres of land of the Matabele people which has no parallel.

The subject of alienation will be dealt with at some length in succeeding chapters of the book.

At this point in time, it is pertinent that a record must be noted concerning the issuing of an Order in Council by the Imperial Government which officially gave Lobengula's territory the name Matabeleland, soon to be followed by another Order in Council that legalized the seizure of tens of thousands of native cattle for the benefit of the Chartered Company and those who assisted in the war effort to subjugate the Matabele.

These two Orders in Council gave the Company power to do as it pleased until 1919 when the Judicial Committee of the Privy Council removed most vestiges of power from the Company to hold 70 million acres of unalienated land as its commercial asset. By the way, it is not quite correct to say power was taken away from the Company because it remained in the Administration until 1923 when it was handed over to the Responsible Government from which Africans were excluded. Therefore, despite the pretence that its power to run things in the two territories had been adversely affected, the Company's power and authority remained unfettered until it surrendered administration of the territories to the white settler so-called Responsible Government. The Imperial Government's winning the land case is therefore misleading because the Company remained the effective administration until 1923 where authority passed on to the Responsible Government. The Crown's winning the land case was therefore effectively a win for the Company.

Under the two Orders in Council Matabeleland was to be ruled by conquest, a contentious subject that forms part of my book *The Rule by Conquest The Struggle in Mthwakazi* which was published in April 2015. The book is banned in Zimbabwe.

In the meantime, the message in the following Order in Council reveals the Imperial Government's evolving new policy:

"*Legally the decision of the Judicial Committee of the Privy Council in the land case does not in any way affect the position of the natives, which is determined solely by the provisions of the Orders in Council. This has been the position ever since 1894*".

These are the words of Sir Henry Lambert in the British Parliament years after the Privy Council decision on the land case.

As far as it is known, there were two successive Orders in Council issued in December 1894. Under the first Order in Council Lobengula's kingdom of Mthwakazi became Matabeleland, while the other ordered the confiscation of Matabele cattle. The excuse offered by the Imperial Government was that the Matabele impis had fired on white subjects of the Crown near Fort Victoria which, under the old order, fell within Lobengula's sphere of influence.

If Sir Henry Lambert's statement quoted above must be taken seriously, the reader can only conclude that the position of the native land remained as it had always been before the conquest of Lobengula. Nothing could be further from the truth because radical and aggressive dispossession of land and cattle were set in motion with the signing of the Secret Agreement on 14 August 1893. From 1914 to mid-1950s expropriation of native land continued unabated with the people in crowded so-called reserves moved to open way for white settlers. We have seen that 672 mercenaries who invaded Matabeleland became the owners of 4 million acres of Matabele land on the day the Secret Agreement was signed. How could the position of the natives on land be determined by the Orders in Council of December 1894? The fact that the orders were based on false claims cannot be over-emphasized.

Of profound interest to the people of Matabeleland,

the only conquered territory to which the provisions of the Orders in Council were applied as a matter of policy is the following:

(a) "All such cattle as were in Matabeleland on/or before the 31st day of December 1893.

(b) The offspring of such cattle as in subsection (a) hereof mentioned born after the 31st December in the year afore said and now in the possession of any native resident in Matabeleland shall be, and the same is hereby, vested in the British South Africa Company. Provided, however, that if any cattle in possession of any such native shall be proved to be the lawful property of any person, not being such native as aforesaid, provision of this section shall not apply, but the onus of proof of such lawful property shall lie, with the person alleging the same'.

It will be shown that the people of Matabeleland, individually or as a nation, lost to the Chartered Company all their cattle, without any hope of having them restored to their lawful owners. The Imperial Government, it was said, only "regularized" what the Chartered Company had started. This raises a whole lot of questions, one which is whether regularizing an injustice was morally defensible and indeed lawful under any British law? The people of Matabeleland might be excused if they raised questions regarding the extent to which this act subverted and compromised British law in order to justify an unlawful act. But the victims were not British people or white men. They were helpless Africans against whom the Imperial Government, the Chartered Company and white settlers were arrayed in a tripartite coalition already referred to in preceding pages of the book.

It will be remembered that one of the clauses in the Royal Charter stipulated in clear terms that one of the reasons the Company petitioned the Imperial Government for the Charter was the promotion of peace and order in Matabeleland, as if peace and order did not exist in the territory before the white man arrived.

This of course was a deceptive and dishonest clause that fooled the Imperial Government to think that granting the petition would prevent the invasion of Matabeleland. Following the preceding Orders in Council, Matabeleland was divided into nine districts and Native Commissioners appointed and given the task of rounding up native cattle at the rate of 200 000 head per month. The operation was not without human tragedy, as the native police exceeded authority in their drive to impress the Company.

Four Matabele women, who could not reveal where the people had hidden their cattle, were murdered. This had terrible consequences that led those who staged an uprising in 1896 to kill every white man, woman and children they could lay their hands on. Insiza District became Emakhandeni, a grisly name created by brutally decapitating heads of the victims.

Cecil John Rhodes was to meet during the Peace Indaba in the Matopos Hills a chief who challenged Rhodes by asking him: 'Who started the killing of women and children?'

A detailed account of this story will be narrated in subsequent pages of this book in which the causes and effects of the uprising will be recorded.

For the moment let the world be reminded that there were 672 white troopers and an equal number of native "bat men" recruited in Mashonaland to invade Matabeleland. While white troopers also stood to benefit to the tune of ten thousand pounds sterling each, there is no known record of a figure for black participants, the bat men.

Another curious omission of blacks pertains to the Roll of Honour of those who fell during the campaign. It is common knowledge that their names are listed in a part of the Bulawayo Post Office building.

This matter, however, will form part of my investigation when dealing with the results of the hunt for Lobengula. That part of this book, most of whose material is drawn from accounts in the book, *The Downfall of Lobengula*. I am an unyielding critic of the fact that the Mashona allowed themselves to join forces of plunder in 1893, only to realize that they had made a tragic blunder.

Seven years after the occupation of Mashonaland they were subjected – together with their professed archenemies, the Matabele – to unprecedented brutality at the hands of the very same people who occupied their territory with promises of protecting them.

But I will defend them against any injustices they suffered at the hands of the Pioneer Column. Mbuya Nehanda believed that Lobengula would one day return to rule the country again. She must have decided that it was better to be ruled by Lobengula than the "kneeless" white people who had hurled sticks of dynamite into caves where her people were hiding.

How else does one explain her and Kaguvi's defiance of these invaders who eventually set up a Kangaroo court that tried them to be hanged and their heads taken to a museum in London? But this was out of character with their welcoming the whites when the latter occupied their land in 1890. Can any argument assert that the Mashona knew that the Pioneer Column would in a short seven years turn against them?

Did Nehanda and Kaguvi's execution provide a fitting propitiation for the future when now the ruling axis of tribalism has adopted a dog-eats-dog syndrome that no longer distinguishes between the Mashona and the Matabele as the ruling party fights to stay in power?

History must recognize that the poor judgment of the situation displayed by the Mashona in 1890 has created irreconcilable tensions between the Mashona and the Matabele. The Mashona have used their foreign military training to oppress the Matabele. They are constantly reminded of the British-Mashona coalition which began with the invasion of Matabeleland. But this book is not about the Mashona-Matabele relations.

It is about the unfinished business of British invasion of Matabeleland in which the Matabele lost everything.

CHAPTER 7

AFTERMATH OF THE SECRET AGREEMENT

WITH the signing of the Secret Agreement, the war began early in October. Details of the operation are not relevant to this book. What must be highlighted are a series of unsuccessful peace efforts by Lobengula which were rejected by the Chartered Company before the invasion and after. There is no known record that the Imperial Government tried to intervene militarily or otherwise, to prevent the slaughter to which the Matabele were subjected with the elderly, women and children found in their kraals bearing the brunt. The book *The Downfall of Lobengula* by W.A Willis and L.T Collingridge (1969) paints a grisly picture of burning kraals but is silent on what happened to villagers who were not fighting the white invaders. Immolation was therefore used to kill everyone found in the kraals in which only civilians were the sol occupants.

Lobengula, however, never gave up on his endeavours to bring about a peaceful end to hostilities, but to no avail. This continued amid growing antagonism between the Imperial authorities and the Chartered Company. Meanwhile, in early October, an agreement was reached between Sir Henry Loch and Lord Ripon that all peace negotiations with Lobengula should be conducted by the High Commissioner, and Sir Henry was ordered to send a message to Lobengula telling him that the Imperial authorities were ready to implement this policy. Any communications from him should promote peaceful relations with the Company. (This approach came too late to stop the war. It also ignores the fact that the Kingdom had already signed two peace treaties with Lobengula). It was made clear to Lobengula, however, that he could not stop forces then arrayed against him.

This approach by the Imperial Government was, however, rejected by the Company, arguing that there was no such provision in the Charter, a Charter whose letter and spirit were being violated by the Company!

Lord Ripon, however, maintained his attitude of supporting this approach, by quoting Clause 7 of the Charter to back up his stand. As already mentioned, that Article of the Charter was based on the Company's petition to bring about "peace and order" in Matabeleland. But the petition had been granted way back in 1889 and the Company now considered that it was no longer obligated to uphold the letter and spirit of the clause as provided in the Charter. This attitude is clear enough from the tone of the Company as expressed by Rhodes in the following telegram to Lord Ripon which was unrelenting:

'The Board of Directors see Marquess of Ripon, ask meaning of Sir Henry Loch's telegram to C. J. Rhodes, stating Marquess of Ripon has placed all negotiations Matabeleland under complete control Sir Henry Loch. The British South Africa Company have asked British Government nothing, and surely they have right, in terms of Charter, if victorious, to settle the question with Lobengula, subject only to approval of Marquess of Ripon'.

Did the Marquess of Ripon approve? If so why? Did the Marquess of Ripon support the move by Chartered Company to invade Matabeleland. Did the people of Matabeleland have any right to question the double standards that were being applied to prejudice the Matabele Kingdom?

This statement by Rhodes suggests that Sir Henry and the Marquess of Ripon were working at cross purposes with the Marquess of Ripon supporting Rhodes. It should be noted that the Charter did not authorize the invasion of Matabeleland. It is clear, however, from the tone of Rhodes' message the Company then felt everything was under its control, and that they no longer needed the authority or support of the Imperial Government or its servants to accomplish their goal. The reader should note that these were the same people whose petition had promised to seek official approval or seek advice of the Imperial Government on the administration of justice and native laws and practices.

At that time, however, the Company was in possession of three key documents, the Rudd Concession, the Lippert Concession and, lastly, the Royal Charter, they ignored what they had promised. But the three documents did not sanction the invasion of Matabeleland. There was, moreover, the Moffat Treaty of amity. What in fact "authorized' the invasion was the Secret Agreement of 14 August of which the Imperial Government was ignorant. In the view of the Chartered Company, therefore, the Imperial Government could now go and hang!

But there is no known record that the Imperial Government protested or condemned such flagrant betrayal of its trust.

We will see in subsequent chapters that the Imperial Government was deeply embedded in the secret exploits of the Chartered Company, and that it later became a member of a tripartite coalition against the natives.

One last thought about the elusive peace efforts on the part of Lobengula. As Capt. P. W. Forbes' forces closed in on him on the Shangani Trail, Lobengula sent back envoys with two bags of gold sovereigns to pacify his pursuers. The men were killed, and the gold sovereigns taken away. He was ready to surrender but, as fate would have it,

Forbes forces failed to capture him, followed by the catastrophe that befell Alan Wilson and his men.

I have already said details of the war are irrelevant to this book. The next chapter, therefore, will focus mainly on the type of weapons that won the Chartered Company the war against the Matabele.

CHAPTER 8

WEAPONRY OF PRECISION AGAINST ASSEGAIS

THE Anglo-Matabele War saga cannot end without showing what weapons were used to lead to such devastating circumstances. Four Matabele regiments were involved in the final Battle of Mbembesi during which the invading forces overwhelmed the Matabele warriors. They were commanded by the legendary Imbizo Regiment Commander, Mtshani who later led the Matabele forces to overwhelm a stubborn Shangani Patrol over almost a day-long combat. Legend has it that Mtshani, in the face of fierce firepower distinguished himself at Mbembesi by grabbing hold of a Maxim machine gun and wheeling it into a nearby pool. Eight graves of those men who were operating the machine gun can be found at Gadade next to the memorial of 6 000 members of the Warriors who perished there in less than a month of fierce fighting. It is almost impossible to fully capture the incredible and devastating formidable odds which the Matabele faced against the British henchmen who bore military machine guns.

The creator of the machine gun, Sir Hiram Stevens Maxim, who invented it in 1885, knew only too well the devastating effects of that weapon.

The Maxim gun was first used in colonial warfare from 1886 to 1914 and was gradually adopted by European armies and navies. It was the weapon of the day in the Russo-Japanese War and World War I, before Americans used it as a training weapon.

It saw service in 25 countries between 1886 and 1959.

The Maxim gun was first used by Great Britain's colonial forces during the 1893-1894 Matabele War in what became Rhodesia.

It was used during the Battle of Upper Shangani by 700 white soldiers who fought off 3 000 Matabele warriors with just four Maxim guns. It played an important role in the swift European colonization of Africa in the late 19th century. Its extreme lethality was employed to devastating effect against obsolete charging tactics, when natives could be lured into pitched battles in open terrain.

As it was put by Hilaire Belloc, in the words of the figure "Blood" in his poem" The Modern Traveller":

'Whatever happens, we have the Maxim gun, and they have not!

The inventor, however, says the destructive power of the Maxim gun in colonial warfare has often been over-egged by popular myth. Modern historical accounts suggest that, while it was effective in pitched battle situations, such as the Matabele war or the 1898 Battle of Omdurman, its significance owed much to the psychological impact the gun had. The original version was capable of firing 600 one-pound shells per minute, and the psychological effect of its sound was awe-inspiring.

This was known in the second Anglo-Boer War as the Pom-Pom from its sound and was used on both sides. The Maxim gun was also used in the Anglo-Aro war of 1901 - 1902 in present-day Nigeria'.

It is pertinent that one must acknowledge the fact that the open-country terrain at Mbembesi was tailor-made for the Maxim gun to produce the devastating results of that encounter. The traditional "scorpion" formation proved a disaster. In the Battle of Lalapansi north-east of what became the town of Gwelo, commanders of the Matabele forces adopted a strategy in which fighters fell flat on the ground to counteract the devastating effect of the Maxim machine gun. This gave the battleground the name Lalapansi whose historical importance has been immortalized to this day.

Official accounts of the war testify to the effectiveness of the Maxim machine gun.

But the bravery that the Matabele forces displayed, as seen from largely partisan accounts in books like, *The Downfall of Lobengula* cannot be allowed to belittle the fighting spirit of the warriors in a hopelessly one-sided war. This is the same war that British forces gave themselves false praise for and which will remain in the annals of history for all time. That this self-glorification frenzy on the part of the British forces was accomplished against a side that was using primitive weapons is often ignored, with the result that praise was given where condemnation should have been appropriate. Also often ignored is the horrifying callousness of the British forces whose policy was to spare no life among the wounded of the enemy. In the popular scheme of things, the world has been robbed of objective accounts of a hopelessly one-sided war in which its colonial prosecutors became heroes of the moment, instead of the villains they were.

There is a side to this war that makes the accounts of the war by settler interest suspect. The reader will recall that 672 Mashona were recruited to fight on the side of the settlers. There is overwhelming evidence, moreover, that their presence in the main was hardly mentioned. If some of them died in the conflict by any means, there is no mention of the fact.

All the world knows about them is the scant reference to "our Mashona" or loyalist natives whenever disaster struck. That their presence was only acknowledged when they were caught by the Matabele forces cannot be denied.

A particularly horrifying incident occurred near Emhlangeni as nightfall forced Capt. Forbes' returning troops to camp for the night. The inevitable laager was erected but the Mashona or loyalist natives were left out to camp 700 metres away. It is explained that Forbes did not suspect that Matabele forces were waiting for them nearby.

The next thing the laagered forces heard were cries of agony as the Matabele forces struck. This leaves one wondering how often the poor Mashona had been left out of the laager in this manner, exposed to the omnipresent Matabele impis. There were still thousands of Matabeles roaming the countryside to attack the enemy where they could, and it was foolhardy for invading forces to take chances. Laxity in taking precautions against the ever-present danger of being attacked had no place under the circumstances. One of the rules of engagement applied by the warriors was speed and surprise which often caught the invaders unaware.

The Battle of Lower Shangani had not demoralized them, and they were to demonstrate this by staging an uprising.

One of the glaring omissions in the official account of the campaign pertains to information as to the fate of villagers whose kraals were reduced to ashes wherever they were found. A report of what happened to the villagers gives a horrifying picture of burnt kraals and a free use of immolation that left charred corpses of victims during the head-long rush from Upper Shangani to Bulawayo when the war began.

As the world knows, the invading forces were to converge in Bulawayo from four points of Matabeleland.

This was designed to ensure that the entire population of Matabeleland was surrounded. Four of the invading forces were based in Fort Tuli and Shashi in the south of Matabeleland, while the two were based in Fort Victoria and Salisbury in the north and northeast of Mashonaland, respectively. The pincer formation again shows that a wide cover of the targeted territory was achievable.

Among the assortment of weapons was the seven-pounder used for artillery work to keep the enemy away. One would think that the invaders were faced with an enemy using weapons of mass destruction in a world-wide conflict.

I have recorded in this narrative my observation of the manner of treatment the Mashona received at the hands of the invaders who involved them in the conflict. Much as I detest their involvement in a war that was not theirs, I will on principle uphold their right to be openly recognized for the role they played. That the settlers failed to recognize in any meaningful manner the Mashona's contribution to the defeat of the Matabele, is deplorable.

One of the burning questions of this conflict pertains to the extent to which the Mashona benefitted. It is pertinent; therefore, that questions are raised as to whether they benefitted at all. It is common knowledge that they shared in some of the king's cattle that were expropriated. But was that all for which they joined the war to kill fellow blacks?

These questions are, of course, raised for academic reasons because the Mashona were not conscripts but willing participants. On Chapter Seventeen of the book *The Downfall of Lobengula*, a memorial in honour of some of the heroes who fell in the Anglo- Matabele war is recorded. In the citation the name of Major Allan Wilson leads the list. Also named in the citation is Captain C. F. Lendy who featured prominently in the Victoria Incident, and was a member of a unit that was led by Major Wilson. Cited among the reasons for the war against Lobengula is the much-publicised protection of the Mashona. The citation also makes a case that portrays the Matabele Kingdom as a threat to other inhabitants in the region. This concocted allegation will be dealt with in following chapters of the book when it will be shown to be totally without foundation.

The citation reads:

"Almost every page of South African history is stained with the bloodshed in a series of wars undertaken to establish the supremacy of the white races, and – it sounds paradoxical, but is nonetheless true – to secure that "Pax Britannica" which is our proud tradition.

(Pax Britannica a proud tradition! And the Mashona lent their hands to the British to enable them to accomplish Pax Britannica's proud tradition.)

"It is, therefore, no small thing to say it seems quite possible that the war lately concluded has finally removed the need for another.
"The Matabele nation constituted the last unbroken military power which menaced the general peace of South Africa; and, as we had already found out in that country, so it proved now: to be a trial of strength and was inevitable."

But there is an element of gross and unfounded exaggeration of the situation in the above-stated claim because it does not show how the Matabele's military power was used to threaten the well-being of South Africa. Is he forgetting that the Matabele had peace treaties with both the British and the Dutch going all the way to 1836?

Why does he choose to gloss over the fact that colonists were indeed responsible for the disturbance and plunder of Africa to please the galleries of their shameless governments? "Apart altogether from Matabeleland, the moral effect of the object lesson among the other native races has been striking: witness the case of Pondoland – till lately the scene of the most horrible forms of savage cruelty – which has been reclaimed to civilization without firing a shot".

Of course, this feat by Pax Britannica, it can be observed, might have been accomplished in Mashonaland where protection of the natives of that territory became the slightest pretext to invade Matabeleland as the object lesson. But the promised protection turned into "the most horrible form of savage cruelty" when the civilizing forces of "Pax Britannica" used explosives to blast Mashona refugees out of caves where they hid from their so-called protectors.

That was the degree of barbarism used to blast the victims as a weapon "to reclaim the victims to civilization without firing a shot". The cost of delivering civilization to Africans in South Africa is indeed studded with horrifying bloodshed. The same, however, cannot be said of Lobengula. There is no iota of evidence that the Kingdom used the level of violence that was commonplace among colonists to subjugate anyone.

This act by British forces turned into a horrible farce when the people of Mashonaland lost the privilege to be "reclaimed to civilization without firing a shot". As for the Matabele, the privilege to be similarly reclaimed to the so-called civilization was cruelly denied them when peace envoys were often murdered to prevent their message reaching the Imperial authorities. The war that was declared against them cruelly became inevitable. The high-sounding message proclaimed by "Pax Britannica", therefore, has a hollow sound of hypocrisy because barbarism by the invading forces was in Matabeleland given a free rein to "teach the Matabele a lesson of their life".

For Pondoland, the people of Matabeleland cannot do better than wishing them Godspeed. There is no known record in history, however, to chronicle to the world Poundland's devastative after-effects of colonialism Because of the absence of such a record, the colonists cannot acquit themselves of wrongdoing in Pondoland.

The same cannot be said regarding the people of Matabeleland whose lives have continued to remain turbulent since the outbreak of the Anglo-Matabele War of 1893. They faced in that year a novel set of circumstances whose effects have not disappeared with the passage of time. The hand of fate was held by their enemies in the form of an arsenal of weapons of precision and heavy artillery which were procured for their destruction. No amount of peace efforts on the part of King Lobengula might have forestalled or halted the determined march to war by forces of the Chartered Company to "smash the Matabele".

As already recorded elsewhere in the book, the Maxim gun pre-determined the winner of that war against which Lobengula did everything in his power to prevent. But no earthly power could stop the "the publicans and sinners" who were behind the war.

The year 1893, the year of the Maxim gun – therefore, became fatal for the people of Matabeleland. No amount of alleged perfidy or ferocity of the Matabele can be claimed as justification for the war. The world is the witness to Lobengula's noble efforts to prevent it. It will be shown in succeeding passages that the motive that drove the British South Africa Company to wage war was, as Lobengula was moved to remark, to rob him of his people and land. The world remains ignorant of the tactics used by the vicious hand of colonialism to get what they set out to get. If the Matabele were misguided enough to oppose Rhodes' expedition, then he and his entourage had every right to use their big guns to win the war, expropriate Matabele land and their livestock to be shared as loot to boot, and the Matabele could go to hell for all their adversaries cared. But there are moral standards that must guide those involved in conflict. The application of those moral standards was totally absent in Matabeleland. The unprecedented episode in the history of colonialism has been justified in the name of civilization. Even the most cynical soul in the universe might stop and wonder how this became possible in Matabeleland. But the world – thanks to "Pax Britannica" – has become immune to the prick of conscience.

The much-claimed British Honour and Justice – once proclaimed from rooftops as the standard to be adopted by the civilized world – have fallen by the wayside. African citizens of the British Empire have become victims of "Pax Britannica", virtues of cynicism and racist bigotry.

The author of *The Chartered Millions, (1920)* John H. Harris makes an interesting observation about the manner in which members of the Chartered Company conducted themselves during the Anglo-Matabele war and after. Because the statement is a reflection of universal concern regarding such evil conduct, it is imperative that one must refer to what Harris had to say. Harris was Secretary of the Aborigines Protection Society who were not allowed to interview Matabele chiefs to establish from their account how the people had been devastated by colonialism.

The following is what he had to say:

"Before entering upon the history of the Chartered Company, let me enter a caveat against the unrelieved picture of wrongdoing in which is often portrayed the work of the British

South Africa Company. The Chartered Company has (in the 1920s) a heavy enough burden to bear, but nothing is to be gained by painting black every individual connected with it and every incident of its development. The Company, like every human institution, has been made up of good and evil constituents. It has been, and still is, splendidly served by some of the lofty-minded men Great Britain has produced, but in the past at least there have been men to whom no act of spoliation and hardly any crime too heinous to commit".

Let me hasten to say the co-architects of the invasion of Matabeleland, Cecil John Rhodes and Leander Starr Jameson exemplified in my view, a bunch of gutter-minded and racist psychopaths, and should not be counted among those lofty-minded men Britain has produced, as seen by Harris. Their characters defied refinement by university education they had acquired. Among Rhodes' followers were men like General Frederick Carrington, who in 1896, ordered passes in and out of Matopos Hills sealed to prevent the insurgents from escaping to avoid the application a policy of extermination of the insurgents and their families who were holed up in the hills during the uprising. Their deserted stores of grain and their cattle were destroyed in a war of attrition to force their unconditional surrender.

Nothing, in recorded history, however, gives a better summary of the case I have tried to portray against the Chartered Company than Harris' remarkable statement. It is even more remarkable when viewed against the fact that the Imperial Government did not condemn any crimes that the Chartered Company committed against the people of Matabeleland. There is, however, a view expressed by Harris against which I must (to borrow Harris' own expression) enter a caveat. The view is marked by the following passage

"... that in spite of notorious misdeeds, flagrant and continued acts of injustice, they (men in its employ) still serve it faithfully from the highest motives of the Directors of the Chartered Company, thereby redeem to a considerable extent the wrongdoing of the past and the injustice of the present".

This statement was recorded in 1920, three years before the Responsible Government.

It is my view and argument that if there was any redemption of the so-called "notorious misdeeds, flagrant and continued injustice" this did not apply to or benefit the victims of the conditions that were created in Matabeleland by the Chartered Company. What was "the wrongdoing of the past (1893) and the injustice of the present" (1919)? In 1893 the British South Africa Company invaded Matabeleland after signing a secret agreement with white settler mercenaries. This led to the expropriation of Matabele land and livestock. In 1919 the Carter Commission of 1914 published its report which recommended the skimming off of the best and well-watered land for the benefit of the Chartered Company and white settlers for all time.

Can anyone talk about redemption of past wrongdoing and injustice of the present under these circumstances? There was, moreover, another aspect of injustice that worsened the plight of the Matabele. This is the rejection of a plea for a protectorate status which was tabled before King George V in 1919. This went down in history as the only case in which a plea for protection was refused the natives in Southern Africa, for the simple reason that the Matabele refused to grant white men the right to effectively occupy the kingdom. They backed this up by defending their country against the invading forces. However, the colonists granted Mashonaland a protectorate status in June 1891 for welcoming the white man on 12 September 1890 when the territory was occupied. This, however, was turned into a monumental farce and meaningless gesture when it came to expropriate native land. The people of Mashonaland suffered expropriation of their land as did the Matabele.

What became a partial redemption (if one might call it so) of the "past wrongdoing and injustice", though, came 77 years later in the year 2000 when the Axis of Tribalism now ruling Zimbabwe launched a revolution that swept away colonial land rights held by 4 000 white farmers. Ordinarily, the land reform programme should have benefitted – as I point out elsewhere in the book – all black people in the country. The opposite has, however, occurred, with the people of Matabeleland lumped together with their white counterpart as foreign settlers to be expelled from the country. The incorrigible Robert Mugabe and his black-on-black apartheid regime simply used the so-called land reform programme as hegemony to occupy Matabeleland. During the first two weeks of 2017 reports surfaced that at least 200 Matabele young men and women fleeing tyranny in Zimbabwe drowned trying to cross the Limpopo River into South Africa. The government of Zimbabwe did not acknowledge the tragedy, let alone offer sympathy to the victims' families or relatives. It reminds one of the Waves of Deaths across the Mediterranean which have swallowed tens of thousands of African and Arab refugees trying to reach Europe. That is the level of hopelessness with which the people of Matabeleland are faced under the Black apartheid regime in Zimbabwe.

Although refugees escaping oppression in Zimbabwe today might feel like the violence of the genocide of the 1980s is no longer their real concern, the policy of tribal exclusiveness being applied against the people of Matabeleland is indeed more brutal than violence because it degrades the very living spirit of the victim. Rather than put up with this treatment, young people every year risk being swept away by swollen rivers and other dangers to become economic refugees in South Africa.

CHAPTER 9

SOUTH AFRICAN NATIONAL CONGRESS PETITION

VERY little is known of the fact that the South African National Congress in 1914 presented a petition to the British Government on behalf of Africans in Southern Rhodesia, which was angrily thrown out. A Congress delegation led by the Reverend John Langalibalele Dube was in London to protest against the South African Native Lands Act of 1913 when the delegation was approached by white leaders of the Catholic Church and the Anglican Church who complained about the manner in which members of their churches in Rhodesia were being treated by the British Government.

The following is the text of the ANC petition presented to the British Government in April 1914:

'The native petitioners are members of the executive of the South African National Congress charged by Congress to visit England for the purpose of appealing to His Majesty to protect the right of African natives over the soil of their native land. The Rhodesian petitioners are resident in Rhodesia who desire to secure for their parishioners in particular, and for the native tribes of Rhodesia in general, equitable treatment at the hands of the British Government. The Reverend John Langalibalele Dube has now returned home for the purpose of conferring with the various Indunas of Southern Rhodesia and arranging for the preparation and presentation of the natives' case. The natives will contend that Ordinances have been made which are inconsistent

with their right in regard to land and that they may rely on the promises of the British Government and that their rights should be preserved to them except in so far as they may have been varied by valid concessions granted in accordance with native customs".

Before I record the response of the British Government to the petition in question, let me note in passing the fact that Reverend Dube was barred from entering the country. I must further record the fact that it was not the British Government that responded to the Petition but the Chartered Company. There is apparently no recorded response by the British Government to a petition which was addressed to it except the fact that the Congress was obliged to drop the projected visit to Rhodesia after Rev. Dube was interviewed by the British High Commissioner to South Africa. The substance of what Dube was told, was not published.

It is noteworthy that the ruling ANC in South Africa has maintained a deafening silence about the plight of the victims of sectarian policies in Zimbabwe which have become a twin of apartheid against blacks that once prevailed in the Republic.

The following is the thunderous response with which the Company, through its Assistant Secretary, recorded its displeasure regarding the petition in a letter to the Under-Secretary in the Colonial Office on 12 August 1914.

"The canvassing of Rhodesia by irresponsible persons with the object of inducing the natives to set up a claim to the land could not fail to have an unsettling effect on the native mind. The natives of Southern Rhodesia cannot be ignorant of the fact that a general European war is in progress, indeed it must be regarded as within the bounds of probability that the area of hostilities may spread to South Africa. The effect of such inquiries would be to convey to the natives the idea that as the white men are fighting among themselves and as certain persons have come to tell them

that the white man's land in Southern Rhodesia really belongs to the natives and that they ought to claim it, the present is a favourable opportunity for getting hold of that land, by force if necessary", read the letter.

The letter does not offer elaboration on what would happen to the natives if they dared attempt to take their land back by force. The veiled threat, however, is there for all to see. The land had already been taken away from them by force anyway and what was the purpose of this indignant outburst? Where did the Chartered Company get the idea that Africans in Rhodesia might consider taking the land from the white man by force? Was this not a far-fetched excuse that the Africans might have considered joining forces with Germans in South West Africa or Italians in the Horn of Africa and Libya, who were involved in the general war among Europeans, against the Chartered Company? The probability was extremely remote. But it must not escape observation of the reader that the outburst by the Chartered Company was intended to intimidate the Imperial Government, and this tactic worked well and Rev. Dube was told to mind his own business and stay out of the land fray in Rhodesia. Dube had been summoned to the High Commissioner's office on the issue.

Whatever the High Commissioner told him was dreadful enough to force him to give up the idea of visiting Rhodesia to meet Africans on the land issue. In April 1914, the Morris Carter Commission was launched and five years later, its recommendations were published, and the Privy Council rejected native claims on the land. So, what in the name of sanity was the Company's Assistant Secretary talking about? And why did the British Government leave it to the Company to respond to the Congress Petition on behalf of Africans in Rhodesia which was addressed to it? What bloody-minded game were the Imperial Government and the Chartered Company playing?

I acknowledge elsewhere in this book the fact that not all employees of the Chartered Company agreed with the Administration concerning the quality and adequacy of land that was ceded to the Africans. I cite the injustice of the Land Apportionment Act as it affected the people of Matabeleland as seen by the Superintendent of Natives in Bulawayo. The views expressed by the SN on the land question were, however, an exception rather than the rule. So what redemption of wrongdoing and injustice was Harris referring to?

It must be left to the reader's imagination the amount of good British public opinion and conscience might assist the Matabele when they submit the bill for settlement of the unpaid debt that has been owed since the land grab of 1893. This accumulated debt can never be settled without the British Crown that won the land claims of 1919. The British Government cannot claim to have succeeded Lobengula without paying reparations and restitution for the damage it inflicted on the people of Matabeleland following the Anglo-Matabele War. There is, additionally, the question of restoration of the kingdom which was declared defunct by the Privy Council. The question remains, of course, as to how the Crown can sustain its claim on the land while at the same time rejecting restoration of Lobengula's Kingdom? It claimed it had succeeded Lobengula. Why must Lobengula and the land not be separated? The British could not succeed Lobengula and throw out his orphans. Only those who were shamefully involved in the sins of colonialism and imperialism could be expected to deny the natives justice in the land question.

In the Report of the Board of Special Reference of the Judicial Committee of the Privy Council, the Crown promised amends but failed to keep its promises to the people. It has over the years exacerbated the matter by transferring power, without involving the Matabele Royal Family, to a party that is hostile towards the people of Matabeleland.

The Nyamande Petition represented both Matabeleland and Mashonaland during the 1918/9 conference which determined the future of land claims from four groups led by the British Crown.

The people of Matabeleland are aware that Great Britain played a leading role in the settlement of the world's most intractable case, the Holocaust Claims for restitution and reparation, long after Hitler had gone to his grave.

The people of Matabeleland know that the money that came from thousands of German companies and Swiss banks, helped to make Israel what it is today. They want, among many other things, the two bags of gold sovereigns surrendered to Paul Forbes by Lobengula in his bid to secure an elusive peace for his country and people.

The world cannot expect the people of Matabeleland to determine the value of what they lost. Under the 1918 Committee of the Privy Council the natives stood to benefit "incalculably" from amends which were promised in that report.

The world at this point in time is still ignorant of the fact that the British South Africa Company went to the Conference claiming ownership of 70 million acres of the people's land as their commercial or private property.

That claim, of course, excluded land which had been claimed by white settlers and multi- national mercenaries that had fought to crush Lobengula's forces and render his kingdom defunct. And the beneficiaries under the Secret Agreement for those who assisted in the invasion of Matabeleland had already taken another 21 million acres of the land.

CHAPTER 10

ORDERS IN COUNCIL AND THEIR MEANING

ACCORDING to John H. Harris, author of the book *The Chartered Millions, (1920)* if Sir Henry Lambert was alive today, and the Rhodesian land question was being revisited and debated in the British Parliament, he would be heard saying

"but I told you in 1919 that the legal position of the land question in Rhodesia lay with those two Orders in Council through which the Matabele and the Mashona lost everything to the coalition of the Imperial Government, the Chartered Company and white settlers".

Was he defending the Orders or simply saying the act of issuing them was legally flawed and, therefore, morally indefensible and that it was a mere act of expediency? If the answer is that the Orders were an act of law, what about the subsequent establishment through a commission of inquiry that they were in fact based on a lie? It was said Lobengula's forces attacked white subjects of the Queen near Fort Victoria in July 1893. Would the establishment of the truth require the Imperial Government to revisit the matter and admit the lie?

In that event, would the law, represented by the British Government, be obligated to recognize an injustice and order a redress to prevent a miscarriage of justice? Moreover, there is another question attached to the issue. If miscarriage of justice was proven, would that require the

Chartered Company to return to the kingdom all the cattle, the land and the gold the Company took away through the authority of the Orders in Council? If not, could this not become a case in which the British law of justice was subjected to subversion to justify an immoral and illegal act that justified an unprovoked military expedition in Matabeleland?

I am not a lawyer by profession and will leave it to the legal fraternity to decide this point. However, I must assert the point that the Orders represented an injustice perpetrated by a "superior" race against helpless natives. It is my view that the matter should have been revisited and the truth established and publicly acknowledged. I am emphasizing this point because I believe that the British ought to be concerned about dispensation of justice in any event or circumstance.

However, it would appear the mission of the Chartered Company and the Imperial Government's supporting role in Matabeleland, and indeed in Mashonaland where the Company was supposed to be there to "protect poor Mashona", was not to dispense or deliver justice. Their mission was driven by greed, avarice and their desire to demonstrate their superiority as a race.

The Imperial Government and the Chartered Company often acted like partners, where the Crown, in issuing the Matabeleland Orders in Council, acted to discharge its obligation to its partner to further imperial and commercial fortunes. The Orders were not an act of God. Someone, therefore, must accept responsibility for their existence. It is not one or the other. Responsibility rests squarely on both.

The charge that this was a racial matter is not a malicious and unfounded accusation to taint or tarnish the supposed good names of the Company and the Imperial Government. The testimony that the mission was indeed to demonstrate the white man's supremacy and punitive intent can be read from the citation in honour of those who died during the Anglo-Matabele War.

The citation is recorded in the Bulawayo Cenotaph, and is quoted elsewhere in this book. That the citation also tells how the English man "reclaimed civilization to Pondoland without firing a shot" is revealing. But then the people of Pondoland, whatever their crime, were not of Lobengula and his Matabele Kingdom.

It is, therefore, an anomaly that whoever drafted the citation should use the example of Pondoland where it is claimed the English men accomplished a rare feat by establishing their outpost of civilization without firing a shot. Was that feat accomplished because the white man reserved the shots for Matabeleland where the invaders committed genocide and other heinous war crimes?

Does the bloody accomplishment in Matabeleland cancel out the glory (so to speak) of the Pondoland experience? However, it must be observed the world is still waiting to hear whether the Pondoland experience was, indeed, accomplished without the British firing any shots.

The Orders in Council created an avalanche of problems for both the Matabele and the Mashona whose effects were felt by the victims for 77 years of colonial rule, and, in the case of Matabele, are still being felt. It took years of a bloody war of liberation to overthrow the colonist and redress some of the grievances of the natives.

It was through these Orders that a process of massive expropriation of land and cattle was set in motion. This process left both the Matabele and the Mashona without security of tenure on land which had been theirs without question before December 1893. The land in question excluded that which had been parcelled out to mercenaries under the Victoria Secret Agreement of August 1893. That was the instrument under which participants in the invasion of Matabeleland became the undisputed owners of 4 million acres even before the invaders crossed the border into Matabeleland to begin the war.

Those beneficiaries under the Secret Agreement, did not wait for the Foreign Office to issue the Orders because the Orders and the Secret Agreement, which was a Chartered Company instrument to usurp land behind the back of its partner, was not the initiative of the Imperial Government. Long before December 1894 Queen Victoria was still trying to stop the invasion. The Company simply ignored her. Rhodes had told Queen Victoria to stop meddling or face an armed confrontation with the Chartered Company's forces. It is pertinent that a question must be asked: did the Foreign Office, in issuing the Orders, forget that the Mashona were a "protected" people and should not suffer expropriation of their land? One can't over emphasise the point that Lobengula or his father Mzilikazi, before him, did not expropriate any land that belonged to the people of Mashonaland.

The traditional British short memory, even though such purported loss of memory is often contrived to render it plausible when Britons are in pursuit of shady or questionable ends among coloured victims of colonialism, is manifest in this regard. It must further be noted that even Mzilikazi's settlement in Matabeleland did not result in expropriation of any land that belonged to the Mashona. Mzilikazi did not interfere with their land as long as they stayed away from his domain. To Mzilikazi, the whole question of ownership of Mashona land before white occupation of that territory was a moral rather than a military issue. Why? Because Mzilikazi had the military power to overrun Mashonaland but chose to do nothing of the sort.

This is a cardinal point that must be borne in mind by those who are tempted to claim that the Mashona occupied Matabeleland before Mzilikazi. It is noteworthy, therefore, that the Mashona waited for 132 years after Mzilikazi's death and 107 years after the conquest of Lobengula before plucking up courage to occupy the domain of Mzilikazi's former Kingdom. This resulted from their acquisition of military experience from their colonial partners; Nuclear power North Korea and Great Britain. It was these two countries that trained the Mashona to commit genocide and ethnic cleansing after Zimbabwe's independence. Did the United Kingdom and North Korea guarantee that, by offering military training to the people of Mashonaland they became the undisputed rulers of Matabeleland? The answer, of course, is that yes, they did because the people of Matabeleland were a military power until the 1893 Anglo-Matabele war. The British and North Korean military training after independence buttressed what the British had started in 1893.

One simply cannot over-emphasise the important historical fact that both Mzilikazi and Lobengula left the Mashona alone to occupy the land which was by choice their domain. The settlement of the Mashona in that territory was not accomplished through war. They found a vacuum and decided to make it their home. But both Mzilikazi and Lobengula respected Mashonaland as a sovereign country and the right of the people of that territory to remain there, while the Mashona, without shame, coalesced with white colonists to invade Matabeleland and helped them to take what was not legally theirs. And to imagine that the Mashona were later to suffer expropriation of their land by the same colonists when they had died supporting the British against the Matabele, boggles the mind.

There, however, must be some people with moral courage within the British system of governance to explain why the natives were treated in this shoddy manner. Can the British people still claim that their national conscience was not violated by a bunch of libertines out on the rampage to make dirty money? To whom was the

Chartered Company accountable? To its shareholders in London, Paris and Berlin who by remote control played the role of a dog in the manger while the rightful owners of the land became nomads being moved from one patch of land to another, land which was held or claimed by absentee so-called owners. I am writing this book for the record only so that coming generations can gain from it the knowledge of the march of history and the so- called advance of civilization in Africa that went terribly wrong.

However, in the colonial brigand's world – it seems – morality was at the tail-end of the brigand's concerns. The standard practice was that the end justified the means. The Privy Council in 1919 ruled that the land had become that of her Majesty's Government. Could this ruling be justified or sustained under any law or authority in force anywhere in the world, except Great Britain?

I am raising this issue because it will be shown that both conquest and the concessions claimed by the Company as their licence to expropriate native land and livestock were not justifiable. This was more devastating to the Matabele than it was to the Mashona. And it is easy to explain why it had to be so. The Matabele, in their tens of thousands, had died fighting against the invaders, and once they were 'smashed' they had to be penalized. There were innumerable numbers of unarmed civilians who were caught up in the crossfire with immolation freely used to burn the victims in their huts.

This was despite the fact that relatively small numbers of the invaders lost their lives in the war, while 6 000 Matabele warriors died at the Battle of Mbembesi alone in less than a month.

What happened to Red Indians in the United States has been quoted by Frederick Courtney Selous in his book *Sunshine and Storm in Rhodesia (1896)* as justification for what happened to the Matabele.

The right of conquest was applied without reservation. The following illustrates how the colonist regarded the rights of the natives in the wake of the invasion as seen by Selous:

"At any rate the lovers and admirers of the Matabele would do well to caution their protégés not to commence another insurrection by the murder of white women and children, for should they do so, they will have cause to rue a war of retaliation, that will be waged with all the merciless ferocity".

The operative phrase in the above statement is that "they will once more have cause to rue a war of retaliation that will be waged with all the merciless ferocity" which had already been committed against the people of Matabeleland.

Selous quotes the massacres of Minnesota in the United States and British suppression of Indians at Secundarabad and other places, as what would happen to the Matabele if there was a recurrence of insurrection in protest against the usurpers of their land. Not many people know what happened at Minnesota or Secundarabad and other native places around the world. But the tone of Selous' promises of exceeding violence is awesome enough to imagine the degree of its ferocity.

This is the same man who held 200 000 acres of Matabele land in the Umzingwani District, and an unknown number of cattle taken from the natives under the Matabeleland Orders in Council.

CHAPTER 11

ORDERS-IN-COUNCIL REGULARIZED

THE Orders- in- Council which "regularized" the invasion of Matabeleland, and the subsequent expropriation of land and cattle in 1894, were, as we have seen, based on lies propagated by the Company against Lobengula. Do the British people – since the British Government cannot be expected to swallow its pride and admit to wrong-doing as manifested by these Orders in Council – care to admit that a calamitous wrong was done to the people of Matabeleland in particular? Can the British Government and people explain to the world why the occupation of Mashonaland (which became a British protectorate) and the invasion of Matabeleland, were both carried out "to protect the poor Mashona" against the Matabele, and yet when it came to the land question "the protected" Mashona suffered as well as the Matabele?

How can the British Government pass the acid test of injustice in which they were actively involved as represented by these instruments of unbridled aggression when in fact the charges against the Matabele that they attacked white men near Fort Victoria before the invasion, held no vestige of the truth?

Every civilized nation, we have been led to believe, has a national conscience, a principle that cannot be subjected to manipulation, subversion or a contrived law of expediency. How could the British people sit there and pretend that their colonial dogs of hegemony, avarice, racist bloody mindedness did nothing wrong in Matabeleland and, therefore, their names should not be tainted?

At a date subsequent to the issuing of the Orders in Council the British Government, through a commission of inquiry, did indeed become aware that there was never any truth regarding the allegation that the Matabele warriors had attacked Capt. Lendy and 18 others near Fort Victoria as alleged? The opposite was, in fact, the truth. If they had indeed attacked the white men, they would have been justified because the King's stolen cattle were found among the cattle claimed by the white settlers. But the warriors were under strict orders not to provoke a confrontation with white settlers in a territory which was still under Lobengula's sphere of influence. Local chiefs were in fact appointed royal herdsmen.

A question that begs to be asked is: Was the Imperial Government willing to revisit the matter and admit that the false charges against the Matabele were a pretext designed to precipitate war to further the aims of colonialism?

Hegemony, avarice and greed won the day when those Orders in Council were issued, and had nothing to do with the Company's world famous mission to 'civilize' the natives or protect the "poor Mashona" who, long before the Privy Council decision, had become subjects of a British protectorate in Mashonaland like any other in Southern Africa.

In this question lay the crux of the matter and whether the acid test to uphold the interest of justice was passed.

Since there is no known record that the Imperial Government ever considered reopening the case, the attitude of the British Government remained anchored on treating the land question in both territories of Rhodesia as having been overtaken by the passage of time. But this was self-delusion at its worst because 77 years, later the white man lost all land rights in a revolution whose results have not been amicably settled as I write, and those who succeeded the expelled farmers are bearing the brunt of heavy land taxes demanded by the new government to finance compensation of the expelled white farmers.

Because the expedition was driven by racial considerations the British Government considered native rights a non-event. What about the hundreds of thousands of Matabele cattle and quantities of gold that the Company took away?

The Orders in Council have been in the British Statutes for at least 120 years now, and it will be argued that the situation has not remained static, and that some change in the land ownership scale must have occurred in the intervening years to bring about a change for the benefit of all the people of Zimbabwe. This is an allusion to the land reform programme of the year 2000.

However, the current attitude of the British Government is that Matabele grievances should be discussed with the black apartheid regime in power in Zimbabwe. To correct or make amends on behalf of the British Government for its wrongdoing? Is this what the United Kingdom is suggesting?

The Zimbabwe land reform programme has not redressed the land imbalance so far as it affected the people of Matabeleland. The good land which was originally taken from the Matabele by white settlers has now been taken by the Mashona.

It is clear, therefore, that the grievances of the people of Matabeleland remain un-redressed. This is due to the fact that the axis of tribalism in power in Zimbabwe has used the land redistribution programme to occupy Matabeleland. Arguments supporting a change for the better therefore hold no value when hegemony has been applied by the very people who partnered the British against the Matabele in 1893, and Britain has continued to give them military support against the Matabele. The simple fact of the matter is that the land reform programme has not therefore been created to benefit the people of Matabeleland but to dispossess and drive them out. They are lumped together with white settlers as foreigners in the land of their ancestors. Our argument is that if white farmers who lost their land must be compensated, so must the people of Matabeleland.

After the Chartered Company invaded Matabeleland the hand of the British Government was once again visible in the post-independence genocidal operations against the people of Matabeleland.

That is the Right of Conquest Madness in Matabeleland that was created by the British Government.

As for the passage of time since the issuing of the Orders in Council, it can be shown that the statute of limitation cannot be applied in cases where violation of human rights is the case. The perpetration of injustice should not be subjected to such limitation, especially where such perpetrated injustice involved the livelihood, happiness and wellbeing of the victims. There is also the question as to whether the Orders in Council were an Act of Parliament which provokes another question: Does an Act of Parliament based on false information bind the perpetrator to ignore the tragic consequences which were unleashed by the Orders in Council that "regularized" the expropriation of land and stock in the name of a flawed "dawn of civilization", with tragic consequences for the victims?

Further, it must be noted that the statutes of limitation did not apply in the case of appropriated land of the Papacy which took 131 years for the land and property to be returned to its rightful owners.

The restoration of vast tracts of land in Europe by Mussolini in 1929 led to the establishment of The Vatican, a sovereign state within the Italian mainland. To the returned land was added the sum of US$21 million in compensation. Why should the statute of limitation apply to the Matabele? This principle established by the Papacy case must be applied in all cases of injustice. The British Government, therefore, cannot hide behind its index finger by passing the buck to its successors in (Rhodesia) Zimbabwe, with whom it committed genocide against the Matabele.

The people of Matabeleland were not British subjects to have been subjected to the whim of British law of expediency to further imperialistic objectives. Had the Matabele won the war, they would have continued to enjoy freedom to live their own life. Cecil John Rhodes and his entourage were not driven away from their homes in the United Kingdom. Their homes were not burned down to force them to find new homes in Matabeleland. These men were driven purely by a desire to acquire material wealth no matter what methods they used to obtain it. No amount of pretence that their mission was to take "civilization" to the natives will change that truth. So, the British standpoint is that the effects of their colonial free-booting enterprise must live for ever among its victims.

CHAPTER 12

PASSING THE BUCK

IT has been said that by issuing the Matabeleland Orders in Council, the British Crown merely "regularised" what had been started by the Chartered Company, but who of the two sides can claim acquittal for the wrongdoing and injustice that were set in motion by their respective roles in this regard? Does regularising an unlawful act make it defensible? And not one of all concerned wanted to remember that the Imperial Government and the Matabele had treaties of friendship and amity 'for all time'. There was further the Royal Charter to back up professions of peaceful intentions granted to the Chartered Company by the Crown and proclaimed as an instrument of peace.

In recent contacts between the British Government and those who are now articulating the issue of restoration of the Matabele Monarchy and homeland, and reparation and restitution to redress Matabele losses in the form of nationhood, livestock and gold, the British government has, however, bluntly passed the buck to the current rulers of Zimbabwe to settle the matter, saying the Matabele Monarchy issue was not raised during the Independence negotiations at Lancaster House. The British government, in an obvious plea of innocence, says the nationalists did not raise the matter in 1979.

Perhaps the British Government has a short memory. From 1914 to 1923 the British Government was talking to the Matabele monarchy led by Nyamande concerning a national home for the Matabele; not the so-called nationalists, not the Responsible Government but the Matabele National Home movement led by Nyamande. It is also a fact of history that the British took the kingdom from the Matabele monarchy and not from the so-called nationalists. And who, therefore, is saying the nationalists, who were preferred by the British Government, were members of Lobengula's family who should have raised the matter? Who, therefore, arranged their exclusion from the Lancaster House Conference but the British Government? The fact that a leading member of the so-called nationalists hailed from the former kingdom should not confuse him with Lobengula's children. He did not represent them, and he would not represent them.

African Nationalism as a rallying philosophy in the fight for self-determination was in vogue then. No nationalist involved in its pursuit was willing to exchange it for all the gold in the world. African Nationalism, or worse still tribalism, promised unlimited power to the nationalists, while Lobengula's children were an undesirable distraction to the British Government whose aim was to surrender Rhodesia to the nationalists. This was a clear case of history repeating itself, from 1919 to 1923 when Lobengula's family was excluded when their land was surrendered to white settlers, to 1979 when they were again excluded from the process that surrendered Lobengula's land to the so- called nationalists.

This was a strategy in which the British Government was working to destroy the memory of Lobengula's Kingdom. It will be shown later how the Matabele Royal family was purged.

But there was a more potent rival to African Nationalism: the element of tribalism which in Africa is responsible for the emergence of more dictators and tyrannical regimes per square mile than can be found in any other part of the world. It was a combination of colonialism and tribalism, therefore, that overthrew

African Nationalism in Zimbabwe and led to the sorry situation in which the people of Matabeleland find themselves today. The adherents of modern tribalism have given it a deceptive but appealing new name: it is called African Democracy. This system of government is licentious, justifies the oppression of minority tribes and offers no appeal to the beleaguered minority groups. It is, therefore, repugnant in the extreme.

The majority tribe must rule, even though such rule must lead to commission of genocide and other crimes against humanity and denial of their human rights. Moreover, the Matabele had committed the sin of perfidy against the invading British forces. In the mind of the British Government, therefore, it had to be either Bishop Abel Muzorewa or Robert Mugabe. We shall see why these two were favoured to rule independent Zimbabwe.

We know how Chief Kayisa Ndiweni, a close ally of the Matabele monarchy, was snubbed by the British Government, insulted, vilified and called names by the nationalists for daring to call for a federal system of government as a compromise.

The nationalists and the British Government were in no mood to let other interest groups contribute ideas for a just settlement outside the framework that the nationalists themselves had sold to the British government as the only way forward. In all this they were encouraged by the British Government whose design was to pass to posterity the thorny issue of a homeland for the Matabele.

The fact that Joshua Nkomo was booted out of a government of national unity after only 20 months in office and was hounded to be killed in his own home and had to flee the country, speaks volumes about the value of this so-called African Democracy. And to recall that his inclusion in the government had been arranged by Lord Soames is a lesson of a lifetime.

The British Government had, strangely enough, made a conditional promise that it was prepared to make amends by allocating money for the benefit of the people of Matabeleland. Using their oppressors? This was on condition that the people of Matabeleland support the then Morgan Tsvangirai-led MDC which would have be used as a conduit through which the money would be channelled for the benefit of the people of Matabeleland! Why was the British Government organizing the people of Matabeleland for Morgan Tsvangirai? Was this another occasion of their contrived short memory to mislead the people of Matabeleland? What difference was there between the birds of the same feather Mugabe and Tsvangirai?

This is a complex and contentious subject and I do not wish to offer substantive argument on it at this stage. But let me observe that the political party concerned is led by allies by ethnicity under the African Democracy philosophy of the ruling Axis of Tribalism in Zimbabwe. The British Government wants to take the value of livestock and gold seized from the Matabele to be disbursed by their mortal enemies!

This is another way of saying the Matabele must support the status quo or forget that the United Kingdom have an account to be settled for the benefit of the Matabele. This is like telling the Jews, for one example, to appeal to Hitler for the settlement of the Holocaust claims. No government in Zimbabwe, no matter how sympathetic (and there is no ghost of a chance there shall ever be one) to the Matabele cause, should become the agent to disburse such money to liquidate what Britain owes the people of Matabeleland. What the British took from the Matabele Kingdom must be re-paid to the Matabele people, not through a third party allied to the axis of tribalism which is responsible for the brutal oppression of the people of Matabeleland.

To return to the subject of the Lancaster House negotiations, first and foremost, it must be noted that restoration of the Matabele Monarchy and homeland was not the Patriotic Front's palaver, if you like, and this, it would appear, suited the British government's plans perfectly. Lobengula's warriors had been disarmed and, therefore, posed no threat that could prove to be a source of worry for the United Kingdom. Three of the King's surviving children who were seen by the Chartered Company as a potential threat to its edifice in Matabeleland were purged by taking them into exile, under false pretences, to die under mysterious circumstances. The place of their exile was under the control of Cecil John Rhodes. And when one of them defied the Company in a bid to return home, a neighbouring British Protectorate was used to deport him back to the Cape Colony.

No chances were being taken to let the princes establish themselves in life among their own people. It goes without saying, therefore, that only the British government had the responsibility to invite all interest groups, including Lobengula's children, to the conference. The British Government was the arbiter in the midst of opposing interests and the British Government chose to preclude the Matabele monarchy from the independence talks. The primary reason for their exclusion owes its place in history to the fact that the Kingdom refused to open the floodgates to allow British invaders of the kingdom without putting up a fight. It is also true that invitation was not extended to them because the nationalists were armed, and the British Government shamefully pandered to their demands. The British Government was intimidated by armed so- called African nationalists.

The dominant so-called Patriotic Front group had their own agenda. They both wanted to rule one country but for different reasons. The one – against all hope – still pursued the once-popular African Nationalism ideal, while the other faction had in 1963 broken away to form an Axis of Tribalism backed by a polyglot of ethnic groups in one half of the country. The avowed mission of the axis of tribalism was to settle old scores with the people of Matabeleland. The failure of the United Kingdom government to invite Lobengula's children to the Conference, therefore, cleared the decks for the settlement of perceived old scores in which Lobengula's people were helplessly on the receiving end. Their exclusion, after Great Britain rejected their bid for protection or homeland exposed them and their people to the vagaries of tribalism.

An important point to remember is that the two "Patriotic Front" factions were in the thick of the Cold War, one backed by the Soviet Union while China backed the other wing. One of the factions, with men trained in conventional warfare, had acquired heavy weaponry including tanks from the Soviet Union which equipment it foolishly flaunted in Zambia for all to see.

The arms, instead of being left in Zambia when ceasefire was declared, were shipped into the country. Whether the reader likes it or not, this, incredibly, was a declaration by this faction that it was ready to shoot its way into power!

This created for Joshua Nkomo and his ZAPU party a six-pronged opposition led by Great Britain, supported by the United States of America, ZANU-PF party, Bishop Abel Muzorewa's party, the Rhodesia Front party and apartheid-ruled South Africa. I advance later in this narrative the argument that shipping heavy arms of war from the Soviet Union into the country added to the formidable array of opposition with which Joshua Nkomo was faced on the eve of the independence elections.

This phenomenon, it will be noted, therefore, added in no small measure to the combined force which was arrayed against him and his ZAPU party. On the other hand,

ZANU-PF, ZAPU'S main rival, responded by keeping its armed cadres outside designated assembly points and used its fighters to mobilize massive intimidation of the population in the eastern districts of the country where, according to Lord Soames, they committed "beastly acts" including shoving iron shafts into their victims' 'whatnot'. The victims were ZANU-PF's own people. There was some feeble talk by British representatives and the Rhodesia Front to ban ZANU-PF from the polls but this, as expected, soon fizzled out after Christopher Soames had a secret two-hour meeting with Robert Mugabe.

Critical observers will also be quick to note that the unwelcome shadow of Umkonto we Sizwe, the African National Congress' military wing, whose members lurked behind bushes in Zambia, Mozambique and Angola to find a springboard in the frontline states to attack white-ruled South Africa, added to the problems with which Nkomo found himself facing.

ZAPU was the only party in the fray which was seriously expected to allow Umkonto we Sizwe to establish bases in independent Zimbabwe to attack apartheid-ruled South Africa. It has been said that Mugabe reached an understanding with the Republic to deny Umkonto Wesizwe the privilege. It is common knowledge, however, that former South African President Thabo Mbeki rushed to Harare from Lusaka soon after independence with a view to negotiate for the establishment of bases for the fighters, but Robert Mugabe outrightly rejected the whole idea.

This coalition of opposition against ZAPU, therefore, ensured that the African National Congress' military wing was denied bases in independent Zimbabwe.

The Umkonto we Sizwe was an ally of ZPRA, ZAPU's military wing. Together they had fought pitched battles against Rhodesian forces in the Wankie National Park in 1967. It was folly for anyone, under these circumstances, to expect ZAPU to win in 1980.

Did South Africa's Defence Minister Magnus Malan and Foreign Minister Pik Botha meet Robert Mugabe in Maputo to discuss Umkonto we Sizwe, as reported in some quarters? The answer will probably remain a secret for all time.

The following remarks regarding the leadership of ZAPU will therefore be unwelcome by many adherents of the party, but one cannot resist the urge to observe in passing that the idea of shipping the heavy Soviet Union weaponry into the country manifested, at the very least, a poor judgment of the situation on the part of the ZAPU leadership. The country, with the forthcoming elections, was hopefully moving into a peaceful environment. What was the purpose of shipping these arms into the country if not to use them against the opposition?

Moreover Nkomo, an ardent nationalist, still expected nationalists in Mashonaland to support his party at the polls. This expectation, however, proved to be ill-conceived. There were simply no nationalists left in Mashonaland on the eve of the independence polls to make any difference for Nkomo and his party. Tribalism had an irresistible appeal to the people of Mashonaland than African nationalism.

There was another facet to the hopelessness of Nkomo's bid for power – the 20 seats allocated to his power base of Matabeleland which were all won by his party. This, however, did not salvage him from the looming decline in his stature as a national leader. His stature was now poised to decline to the level of a mere provincial leader. For a man who had staked his political career on the euphoric appeal of the subject of African Nationalism, this development was agonising enough for him. It is, therefore, understandable he chose to capitulate to the Axis of Tribalism in 1987.

History, however, will judge him harshly for this

whopping betrayal of the people of Matabeleland and the Midlands whose faith in his leadership was overwhelming. That the signing of the Unity Accord was indeed a betrayal cannot be denied. There are two episodes in Nkomo's life that also must have impelled him to "commit political suicide" by destroying the name of ZAPU in 1987.

Both incidents occurred during the days when he had become a fugitive on the run from the vagaries of extremist sectarianism following his February 1982 removal from the government of national unity. Both of these episodes threatened his life.

He was returning from Shonganiso School in Chief Murinye's area of Masvingo where he had been invited to be a guest of honour at the official opening ceremony of the school. His host was none other than its founder, Jonas Zvobgo, Edson Zvobgo's father. Edson Zvobgo was one of Nkomo's unyielding critics. This did not, however, stop senior Zvobgo – a lifetime ZAPU member – inviting Nkomo to the occasion.

Nkomo was accompanied at the ceremony by Titus Mhetu of Zaka and Joseph Ndebele, a Bulawayo resident. They were returning from the ceremony and were driving through Masvingo City, past one of Edson Zvobgo's public houses, when a mob spotted them and tried to lynch them by stoning them to death, shouting 'Ngomo, Ngomo uyo' as they rushed to block the vehicle. The driver however, remembering his defensive driving skills, managed to evade the screaming mob. Nkomo had lost the support he had once enjoyed in this part of the country.

Vice-President Phelekezela Mpoko accused the MDC leader Morgan Tsvangirai of involvement in the incident. The trouble, however, is that the only thing of good report about Phelekezela "Report" Mpoko is that he earned his job as Second Vice President by defecting from Nkomo's party. He cannot therefore pretend he is such a great supporter or admirer of Joshua Nkomo. Vice President Mpoko, as

Deputy Director of Demobilisation, was there when a sectarian brigade was formed to commit genocide among his own people. Many can testify to the fact that a number of the victims were his blood relatives. This subject is not about politics. It is about history, the record of what happened in that bloody, tragic and calamitous episode in the history of independent Zimbabwe in which innocent civilians were slaughtered indiscriminately.

The second incident, of course, is a well-known one which happened when units of the 5th Brigade surrounded Nkomo's Pelandaba home but found he had escaped minutes earlier. Nkomo has told the world that three members of his household were killed, and a vehicle parked in the yard had its windshields shattered. Nkomophobia was exploding. He says he fled the country because he feared for his life. For hours before he left his home a light aircraft had been flying over the black western suburbs of Bulawayo warning the residents not to attempt to escape as members of 5th Brigade patrolled on the ground. A voice could be heard from the aircraft saying, "You are surrounded". But Nkomo had just slipped out of his home as units of the army burst into the yard and started shooting indiscriminately. Three men who were sleeping in the house took fatal shots. This was in 1982, five years before the signing of the Unity Accord. This frightful episode was enough to make Nkomo change course after returning from the UK where he denied the situation in Matabeleland and Midlands was tribally inspired.

A story is told about how Nkomo, after his return from the United Kingdom, announced his decision to join the ruling ZANU-PF party. The announcement, at a meeting in a Red Cross Hall in Bulawayo's high-density suburb of Njube, was attended by Joseph Msika, John Nkomo, and Naison Khutshwekhaya Ndlovu among others. According to eyewitnesses, without a preamble, the ZAPU leader announced: 'We are joining ZANU'. It was an order. There was a long silence before John Nkomo offered dissent, saying that was out of the question. This provoked Msika to stand up, threatening to beat John Nkomo up. "You are responsible for what we are today. You are Mugabe's ear here, and you want us to die", charged Msika.

Joshua Nkomo weighed in: "Mugabe says we shall die if we don't join his party". Snap! ZAPU had finally and truly become "a dead donkey", and this smelly description of the party did not come from Callistus Ndlovu this time.

He is the man who coined this unpalatable description of ZAPU as he walked out to join ZANU-PF in the early days of independence. This time it was Joshua Nkomo himself who announced the move to destroy his own party, and the decision to destroy ZAPU was final. The decision was not taken by the decision-making arm of the party. Perhaps this explains why the great majority of party members and supporters remained loyal to ZAPU until after his death when they moved to join the newly formed Movement for Democratic Change. Their movement from the MDC to the ruling party is a long subject but it is due to persistent intimidation and coercion and the people found themselves in the deep end of despair. The people of Matabeleland suffered cruelly from the government's applied policy of exclusion against the people.

It is sometime a good thing to capitulate. But capitulation to tribalism cannot earn one a decoration, when the move exposes one's own people to vagaries of rabid tribalism and the march towards a one-party state. Leading a party like ZAPU, it must be admitted, was an extremely difficult exercise. It had gradually declined from being a national organization to that of a regional one.

Nkomo, however, strongly believed ZAPU had a viable future because of the appeal that African Nationalism had enjoyed until 1963 when a tribally based opposition in the name of ZANU was formed. He had, over, the years surrounded himself with supporters from

Mashonaland. But this support began to dwindle with defections from the party.

By the time the country braced itself for the 1980 elections, only a handful of Nkomo's supporters from Mashonaland region remained. But their children were no longer with them, moving enmass to join ZANU. It was a painful experience for Nkomo.

Let us return to the subject of the Matabele Monarchy. The British government, on the other hand, faced with armed surrogates of the Cold War, therefore, chose to deal only with those who held arms of war to demand independence, at the expense of Lobengula's children. To say they were excluded because of failure by the nationalists to raise the alarm on their behalf, is a British government gambit designed to silence criticism.

The British government's Grand Plan to ensure that there was no further resurgence of calls for the Matabele monarchy or homeland, remained intact. If allowed a hand in the negotiations, the presence of any of Lobengula's children could turn out to be an embarrassment. The leader of the proponents of a Matabele national home was long dead, another phenomenon that added to the British Government's peace of mind in this regard.

The legitimacy of such a call could not be side-stepped or ignored. But there can be no running away from the fact that Britain designed that Lobengula's children – those of them who were still alive - should be left out. There is overwhelming evidence moreover, that those of them who died in exile, their deaths were engineered by the Chartered Company.

And yet in the eyes of the British Government, their exclusion represented a minor thorn in its flesh, and it was decided to do business with what the British Government saw as the lesser of many evils and the two PF factions won the day.

But one cannot close the subject of ZAPU's heavy arms

of war in the assembly point without mentioning the power of tribalism, the all-conquering instrument of the Axis of Tribalism to which Bishop Muzorewa's UANC added its support to bolster the power base in the ethnic scale. It is common knowledge that Muzorewa's *dzakutsaku* militia was armed by the Rhodesian government. This combination of anti-Nkomo forces sealed ZAPU's fate.

On the other hand, the Matabele national home issue was a facet in a game which played itself out in the arena of the Cold War in which Lobengula's children were not involved. But if it was not expedient to invite them why was it necessary to invite Bishop Abel Muzorewa and Ndabaningi Sithole? The answer is that both the Rhodesian Government and the British Government believed Muzorewa would win the elections to form a proxy government of independence in Zimbabwe. Muzorewa, however, did not have any legitimate claim to represent anyone in the country. The expectation for him to win had been given a fillip under the short-lived Rhodesia-Zimbabwe dispensation of which Abel Muzorewa was leader with Ian Smith.

The United African National Council, formed after the banning of ZAPU and ZANU, united the African people (so it appeared) behind Muzorewa. It was Muzorewa who appointed Simon Muzenda and John Nkomo to represent the UANC in Zambia where they immediately separated to join ZAPU or ZANU, respectively. But in the calculation of both the British and the Rhodesian government, Bishop Muzorewa's showing during his term as the head of the Rhodesia-Zimbabwe government was seen as an indicator that the clergyman had emerged from the dark closets of his church to the limelight of popular political support of his African people to beat both ZANU-PF and -PF-ZAPU.

But the idea of a proxy government in Zimbabwe, had

they been invited, could not be seriously considered in the case of Lobengula's children who had demanded a national home of independence for the former kingdom. The British Government saw any presence of Lobengula's family as a complicating nuisance which had to be avoided. After all, the grand plan was to obliterate for all time from the annals of history anything that smacked of a desire to restore the Matabele monarchy. ZANU-PF and the British Government's long-term plans were identical and were designed to keep the Matabele out of any future government of the country. These designs were to be hugely boosted by Joshua Nkomo's signing of the famous Unity Accord in 1987. This was the infamous culmination of his expulsion from government of national unity back in 1982. From then on, the people of Matabeleland became "dissidents" to be hunted down, and henceforth they have become victims of cruel exclusion from the good of belonging.

The move to capitulate by Nkomo sealed the betrayal of the people of Matabeleland and the Midlands, so much so that their mortal enemies, the the Axis of Tribalism, can today sing their swan song 'Nkomo *mudara wedu*' (Nkomo is our old man). What did the man do to earn this accolade when in 1982 Robert Mugabe called him a snake in his government before throwing him out? Nkomo then became a fugitive who escaped death by leaving the country.

The answer to this question comes from ZANU-PF architects of the Grand Plan who say Nkomo, by signing the unity accord, committed political suicide. "Nkomo mudara wedu" therefore, is not a love song. And where does one put the chorus "Nkomo karikamombe" in this swan song when a monument belittling him as a "little cow" still stands in the form of a public building in a square for all and sundry to see and have a good laugh?

The proclamation by the Imperial government in 1919 that it had succeeded Lobengula and held the land in trust but was unwilling to restore the kingdom to Lobengula's children, was lame, opportunistic and, in argument, unsustainable, representing as it were the best of both worlds. The exclusion of Lobengula's family, therefore, was contrived. But there was this comforting thought for the British Government: if the subject arose in future those responsible for their exclusion from the talks at Lancaster House would be long dead and happily buried to be called to account. The issue about Lobengula's children had, by 1979, reached a dead end, to United Kingdom's glory. This is what the British government has chosen to do to perpetuate the issue by passing the buck to those who had nothing to do with what the British government itself created to be a subject of controversy for posterity. The British Government's attempt to use this tactic to avoid its accountability in the Mau Mau claims case is well known.

That the people of Matabeleland are living that painful posterity which has led to the commission of genocide against them is no concern of the British government, it would appear, even though Great Britain's hand is visible in two genocides against the people of Matabeleland in the last century. Must that be swept under the rug to be forgotten?

It is accepted that genocide charges against the United Kingdom perhaps cannot be sustained in any international court of law. This is because those who committed war crimes against the Matabele in 1893 cannot be summoned from their graves to appear before the International Court of Justice.

This also applies to 100 or so faceless officers who provided military training for the unit in Zimbabwe that committed war crimes during the eight-year Gukurahundi campaign in Matabeleland and the Midlands. But the ten-year military training stint of the Zimbabwe army by British military experts at their base in the Nyanga Highlands is well documented and some of the officers who recruited a sectarian force from the ragtag of ZANLA forces are well known.

Capt. Chuck Ivey of the British contingent assigned to train Zimbabwe's 5th Brigade told a BBC reporter on camera that the Government of Zimbabwe could not tolerate what "is happening in Matabeleland" just as the British Government had not tolerated what happened in Northern Ireland. This was a politically motivated statement by a member of the British military top brass in Zimbabwe to train that sectarian force.

It is also common knowledge that a Zimbabwean was sent to Sandhurst for specialized training before returning home to command 5th Brigade for operations in Matabeleland and the Midlands. This facility was like naming a British officer to command 5th Brigade in Matabeleland.

The only difference was that the so-called dissidents in Matabeleland and the Midlands were created by the Government of Zimbabwe to justify genocide among innocent civilians.

The British Government's culpability is highlighted here for the record because it is true but charges of genocide against the British are probably unsustainable.

But the same cannot be said about the outstanding case of reparation and restitution in which the British Government alone must be accountable. The United Kingdom Government and other champions of invasion of Matabeleland are still on the warpath against the Matabele for the crime of alleged perfidy. This apparently is where the British Government wants the whole shameful business to end.

The British have not weaned themselves from the Matabele phobia that has characterized their relationship with the Matabele people for standing up against them in 1893. But what is the standing of the right of conquest in international affairs today when a superpower can join another to give a dictatorship military support to commit genocide?

The most shameful truth is that the British government became bedfellows with North Korea in the training of those who were employed to carry out genocide against the Matabele to settle perceived old scores.

That this reign of terror in Matabeleland and the Midlands has since become a dog-eat- dog in Mashonaland itself, as Robert Mugabe tried to extend his hold on power by installing his wife in his place to create a Gushungo Dynasty of dictators, this created intolerable conditions in Mashonaland itself. And Mugabe's tipped successor, Emmerson Mnangagwa was reported in 2013 as telling villagers attending an election rally in support of his wife in his home area that he went abroad to be "trained to kill" is dreadful to the people of Matabeleland, and indeed to the people of Zimbabwe as a whole.

He is the man who was responsible for State security during the massacres in Matabeleland and the Midlands and is not ashamed to tell his own people he will kill them if they do not vote for his wife. What is left in Zimbabwe to give satisfaction to the powerful? Massacres and more massacres perhaps! Enforced disappearances and things like that perhaps? Is it a culture of violence against the opposition and minority groups perhaps?

Zimbabwe's human rights record continues to be a subject of concern, with the country named as one of only two African countries where violation of human rights is still a cause for concern within the international community. What perhaps is another subject of concern is that the 2013 Constitution is being subverted "with impunity", according to *The Legal Monitor*, which is published by Zimbabwe Lawyers for Human Rights for members and human rights defenders.

According to the newsletter, Zimbabwe has since 2011 appeared before the UN Universal Periodic Review (UPR) which is based in Geneva, with Vice President Emmerson Mnangagwa leading a strong delegation of government and party stalwarts to Geneva twice since 2011 to defend the Government's human rights record.

So, it was decided in 1979 that potential proponents of the subject of self-rule for the Matabele, represented by Lobengula's children, should not be allowed a chance to argue the merits of their case at Lancaster House.

One of the dreaded questions that Lord Carrington faced was "how could the Imperial government assert its claim to have succeeded Lobengula and at the same time refuse to restore to the king's orphans the symbol of their national identity, if the idea was not to obliterate the monarchy from history?"

The British Monarchy, through the decision of the Privy Council, had in 1919 declared itself the custodian of Lobengula's children, and that it held the land in trust. It could not morally hold the land in trust for white usurpers. And yet it did exactly that to the exclusion of the real owners of the land.

The Imperial Government held the key to solving the problem of a homeland for the Matabele. How, for instance, was it possible that the Matabele Monarchy had become exchangeable with that of the British Crown without making it possible for the glory of the Matabele kingdom to be restored? Furthermore, the shameful subject of concessions and conquest, which were being proffered as licence to invade the kingdom, were not sustainable and the concessions had in fact been repudiated, the Lippert Concession by decision of the same Judicial Committee of the Privy Council and the subject of conquest by failure in 1893 to apprehend Lobengula. It was unthinkable, however, in the view of the British government, that Lobengula's children should be invited to the conference. That sealed the subject for posterity.

CHAPTER 13

NYAMANDE THE ENIGMA

THE Matabele monarchy is a closed book to most people in this country. Even less known to the general public is King Lobengula's eldest son, Nyamande, the man who articulated to have both his father's crown and kingdom restored but was frustrated by those who administered Matabeleland after Lobengula's disappearance.

This is the man who founded the Matabele National Home Movement. This is the same man, more than any other, who drafted a petition for submission to the Imperial Government calling for a national home for the Matabele. That he failed to persuade the British government can hardly be blamed on his inability to articulate the subject. His failure to achieve his goal can squarely be blamed on the Imperial Government's inflexible stance which was closed to any idea of a homeland for the Matabele. This became part of a design to obliterate from history the legacy of the Matabele Kingdom. I shall deal later with the subject pertaining to the purging of the Matabele Monarchy.

It was restoration of the monarchy, more than anything else that promised the Matabele dignity which had been theirs under the Kingdom, instead of perpetual humiliation which became their lot, and continues to be the lot of the people. For the reader to understand and appreciate the negative historical background which stood in Nyamande's way in his pursuit of restoration of the monarchy, reference must be made to the 1896 uprising in which he played a leading role. This was a conflict during which more British men, women and children lost their lives in a lightning move by the insurgents than had been accounted for during the 1893 Anglo-Matabele war. Had Cecil John Rhodes not intervened by negotiating peace with the insurgents, Nyamande would have faced trial and certain death for his role in the uprising. He was among those who were on the list of proscribed insurgents for trial in a kangaroo court to be hanged or shot. It goes without saying therefore that his attempt to create a national home for his people was considered an affront which was totally unacceptable to the British Administration in both Southern Rhodesia and the United Kingdom.

Many of his colleagues in the uprising were tried and hanged for their involvement. That he escaped death can only be due God's hand. But he emerged from insurgency to become a rallying figure for the creation of a homeland for his people.

His failure to achieve his goal was despite the fact that he sought to create a national home for the people within the framework of British protection as granted to Barotseland, Basutoland, Swaziland and Bechuanaland. The British South Africa Company was the Administration in both Northern and Southern Rhodesia at this time. The only rational explanation for his failure to persuade the Imperial Government to grant him his desire is that he was a radical as much as he was Lobengula's son. The British were unyielding in their opposition to Nyamande as a rallying figure for the restoration of the Kingdom. This explains, therefore, why the people of Matabeleland were singled out for exclusion from the community of British-protected territories in the region. It explains why Nyamande failed to achieve his objective.

It is true, therefore, that the rejection of his proposal owed its failure to the crime of perfidy of which the Matabele had been accused ever since the Company started preparations to invade and smash their kingdom to "'to teach the Matabele a lesson of their life'".

If refusal to open the flood gates to invaders is a crime, then perfidy was indeed the crime for which the Matabele were violently suppressed and persecuted and continue to be persecuted to this day.

Rhodes is on record as telling the world that the only roadblock against his ambitions was Lobengula. This explains why Matabeleland was in 1923 annexed to form Southern Rhodesia with Mashonaland. The annexation was the first move in Great Britain's grand plan to ensure that the Matabele were denied a national home for all time.

The Imperial government, in their pursuit of this grand plan that reached its climax at independence, had to punish the Matabele rather than give them the pleasure of a homeland, let alone becoming protected subjects of the British Crown.

The British, in 1979, crafted a constitution that gave their man the edge to win the 1980 elections. The winner represented the tribe that welcomed the colonial occupation of their territory in 1890. These were the same group of people, who, at independence were to receive British military training to launch an unprovoked military campaign "to deal once and for all" with the so-called Matabele question. Is the so-called Matabele Question now a dead subject because the United Kingdom and the black apartheid regime have swapped places in Zimbabwe? Not at all!

But how could anyone in his right mind expect the British to forget that the "perfidious Matabele" fought and died defending their territory, killing untold numbers of British kith and kin in the process?

It will be shown how, as the Imperial government prepared the ground to surrender the booty of the so-called conquest to white settlers at the end of the First World War, and the people of Mashonaland did not articulate any protest against the British move. Why should they when

Britain was there to protect their interests which, in a cruel paradox, Britain failed to discharge! Can anyone trust Great Britain's rationality and consistency in any event?

The British must stop the pretence that power politics has anything to do with right and justice. If right and justice were the standard that guides their actions in a world in which they have played a leading role in causing the turmoil that grips many parts of the world today, they would have granted the people of Matabeleland a homeland which was their right. Instead the Matabele have been subjected to genocide in which – not once – the hand of the British is visible.

In the Rhodesian land debacle, the Matabele again found them-selves alone to oppose the move to surrender 70 million acres of the so-called un-alienated land to the white invader-settler community.

It was natural that they should call for creation of their own homeland, and the leader of the movement that spearheaded the call was Nyamande. The movement remained potent and focused long after Nyamande had died around 1929.

Terence Ranger in his book *The African Voice in Southern Rhodesia (1970)* says Nyamande, uneducated though he was in the western sense, had "turned out to be quite an effective leader" under the environment that prevailed in the territory. He quotes the Superintendent of Natives in the Chartered Company Administration as describing Nyamande as having "a doggedness of purpose that may achieve more than is desirable". What was undesirable was the creation of a Matabele national home. So, nothing was spared to ensure that his national home dream was condemned to remain nothing but a mere dream.

There was unrelenting opposition from both the Imperial Government and the Company which had forced

Lobengula to flee the country in 1893. Nyamande faced threats to remove him from society altogether, like his three younger brothers who died ignominious deaths in Cecil John Rhodes's domain of the Cape Colony to where they had been exiled to destroy the Matabele monarchy. Nothing was being spared to force Nyamande to abandon his national home enterprise.

His opponents formed a formidable coalition that could not be shaken out of its anchors of abused power. Nyamande's crime was that he was a stubborn driving force behind the Matabele National Home movement which attracted support from among people of all walks of life in Matabeleland.

But Nyamande for a long time was unmoved by these threats and remained scornful of loyalist Indunas who were being consulted by the Administration, describing them as mere *"abantu bokukonza"* (mere praise singers) "who know nothing about the Matabele national affairs".

These were indunas who were being used to drive a wedge between him and his father's people. He once told the Administrator of Rhodesia that had Lobengula won the war *"my father would not have starved the surviving Englishman ..."* as he was being starved by the invaders of his country to humiliate him. He had been crowned king in June 1896 and, after his surrender following a general amnesty, followed by his appointment as senior chief for Bulawayo District. This was a move to depose him which he rejected and was kept in a fenced 'keep' away from his people where he died a recluse.

His grievances had developed from being personal to embrace the grievances of the Matabele in general.

The Administration, therefore, adopted a strategy that ensured he failed in his bid for a homeland. These tactics did not end with just driving a wedge between him and the renegade chiefs but threats to remove him from society increased. This tactic included giving his opponents among chiefs some of his father's remaining cattle while he complained of "poverty and hunger". He asked the Administrator if at all the Company cared about his loyalty.

He got a very lame answer: *"You have asked me to give what is not in my power to give"*, said the Administrator. But the Administrator was a policymaker who chose to fob Nyamande off with a glaring excuse instead. What the Administrator was saying was that his power was limited to taking land and cattle from the Matabele and nothing else, and not giving some back!

This, however, did not diminish Nyamande's determination and he consulted widely all leading chiefs and other members of the former kingdom by writing letters to them for their opinion. *"It is not war, Oh People!"* Nyamande declared to allay their fears that he might be working to drag them into war with the Company. His popularity was increasing and so was the support for a homeland. The Administration was getting concerned and it was decided that he should be bought off by offering him ample land of his own within the confines of a native reserve.

That approach, however, was abandoned after the Chartered Company discovered that Nyamande had written several letters to the Kingdom's indunas in which he stated that he called for two-state solution. He strongly argued against armed insurrection against the Administration but was pursuing his call for a Matabele National Home where the full benefits of self-government would be established and enjoyed.

His approach was a proposal to the Administration to have the territory divided between his people and the white settlers. This arrangement would gain for Matabeleland the status of a British protectorate. It will be shown that the proposal was contemptuously rejected by both the Administration and the Imperial Government. It was feared this would have saved the Matabele the punishment that the British intended to meet out against them. The grand plan was to terminate for all time the Matabele monarchy's lineage to forestall future calls for its restoration. This involved taking Lobengula's male children to exile where an attempt to indoctrinate them against the idea of restoration of their Kingdom failed, forcing the Company to resort to destabilizing them which led to their early death.

This proved to be a turning point which eventually led to the 1919 decision of the Privy Council that rejected, not only the call for restoration of the kingdom but also any claim on land and livestock the Matabele might attempt to make.

The Privy Council decision (for the time being) placed on the same level the Company, the Africans and the settlers as mere claimants of the 70 million acres of unalienated land. In terms of the Privy Council decision the land became the property of the British Crown, to become the property of the envisaged future government of Southern Rhodesia. This represented a whopping victory for white settlers and a victory for settlers was a victory for the Chartered Company. It was a victory that was immensely facilitated by the Imperial Government with its legal arm putting a seal of finality to the land question.

Responsible Government, still five years away in 1923, loomed in the horizon and the Imperial Government was frantically preparing the ground to hand over the administration of the country to a future white government of Southern Rhodesia.

The Imperial Government could no longer pretend they did not know who was to become the Responsible Government in the conquered or occupied territories. Already a fierce debate was under way to decide whether Southern Rhodesia should join the Union of South Africa.

This was a debate from which the dispossessed natives were excluded. Leading the opposition to the idea was a brilliant Irishman named Charles Coghlan, a lawyer by profession who became the first Prime Minister of Southern Rhodesia. He is the same man who will be seen representing the people of Mbembesi on the land issue. They lost not only the land - land donated to them by Rhodes as reward for their role in the pacification of hostilities of the Matabele uprising, but also their money paid to Coghlan in legal fees.

Meanwhile, white mercenaries who helped to invade Matabeleland had since December 1893 taken 21 million acres with no questions asked. It is noteworthy that the natives who supported the successful invasion campaign were not entitled to any land under the Secret Agreement, and indeed got nothing under that agreement. Instead they lost all their fertile and well-watered land and were forced to live on rocky pockets of land between mountains.

It can be shown, therefore, that the occupation of Mashonaland and the subsequent invasion and conquest of Matabele Kingdom was purely a racial matter with no other merits, except of course what these so-called "publicans and sinners" stood to gain for the British Empire and themselves. As far as the Privy Council was concerned the natives of the two territories could go and jump into the deep blue sea for all the highest legal body in the British Empire cared.

Let us therefore go back to the decision of the Privy Council which, it can be shown, marked the first time that the Imperial Government actually admitted responsibility for the shambles that was wrought by the occupation and invasion of the two territories of Southern Rhodesia. It makes nonsense of Queen Victoria's assurances to Lobengula that Her Majesty's government had no intention to invade Matabeleland or drag him into war. And indeed, it makes nonsense of all those peace treaties with Lobengula that purported to promote peace and friendship between the two nations. As it will be seen in the unfolding cruel paradox, it was to be Queen Victoria's grandson, Prince Arthur of Connaught who delivered the last deadly blow against Nyamande's quest for restoration of the Matabele monarchy and his bid for a homeland.

CHAPTER 14

NYAMANDE'S SOUTH AFRICAN CONTACTS

NYAMANDE'S efforts to bring back his father's kingdom owe a great measure of their impact to the role played by his advisors recruited from the ranks of blacks from South Africa. In 1912, only two years away from the institution of the Carter Commission to finally decide the land question in Southern Rhodesia, the South African Native National Congress was formed, and among its inaugural conveners was Alfred Mangena, the first black barrister to practise law in South Africa. Mangena, after Professor John Langalibalele Dube was barred from entering Matabeleland to meet Nyamande, became the first man from the Congress to do so in an endeavour to give him political and legal advice, only for him to be deported from the territory as an agitator before accomplishing his mission.

According to Prof. Terence Ranger in his book *The African Voice in Southern Rhodesia*, Mangena then assigned Richard Msimanga to take his place. Msimanga was the son of the founder of the Independent Methodist Church of South Africa who recruited another clergyman, the Rev. Henry Reed Ngcayiya, leader of the Ethiopian Church of South Africa, which was now well-established in Matabeleland, to visit Nyamande.

Among leading figures already resident in Matabeleland from the Eastern Cape who became involved in the land question in Matabeleland in particular were people like John Hlazo and Chief Garner Sojini, and clergyman John Ngono among others.

Hlazo and Sojini led Mangena to Nyamande. The movements of these men were under the watchful eye of the Adminisration, and Ngcayiya pretended he was visiting a cousin, the Reverend Radasi on Church business while his real purpose was to meet Nyamande and help draft a petition on his behalf to be submitted to the British authorizes led by King George V.

There was a community of people from the Eastern Cape at Mbembesi, some of whom had come from the Colony as wagon drivers and had fought along the British against the Matabele in the 1896 uprising. Rhodes had rewarded them with pieces of land in the Mbembesi area and they gradually became disillusioned with what they saw as a litany of unkept promises by the Chartered Company after Rhodes' death. Their prominent leaders were Chief Garner Sojini and John Hlazo. Although Hlazo had purchased land from the Company in the vicinity of Mbembesi and managed to pay up front for it, being, however, denied title as promised by the Administration, Sojini was not so lucky and was forced to leave the area for Selukwe where he leased a piece of land and became a prosperous farmer. While living in Mbembesi he was not recognized as a Chief, a position he enjoyed when he and his people were taken from the Cape with promises to provide and secure title in their newfound home. Happy though he was in Selukwe where he leased land from a white settler land investment company which traded under the name of Willoughby Concessions with holdings across several districts of Matabeleland, Sojini had grievances because the Chartered Company refused to sell land to him although he had money enough to pay for it up front. He felt that Rhodes' promises had been broken, forcing him to become an agitator against the Company.

The concession company belonged to Sir John

Willoughby, one of the pioneers who led the Salisbury Column to invade Matabeleland in 1893.

Hlazo became a bitter opponent of the Administration due to its failure to give him title to the land which had been allocated to him but was denied title to it. Both Hlazo and Sojini resorted to hiring a lawyer named Charles Coghlan to fight the Administration.

Coghlan was ambivalent, wanting to help Hlazo and Sojini but being inhibited by self-interest. He was a leader of white settlers who were strongly opposed to the idea of a union with South Africa and, as already said, was to become the first Prime Minister of Southern Rhodesia in 1923. The issue of joining the Union of South Africa was seen by white settlers as a danger that would lead to the granting of protectorate status as demanded by Nyamande. The Union of South already had four such states. This possibility therefore must have weighed heavily in favour of staying out of the Union. There is overwhelming evidence that uppermost in the minds of the Chartered Company administration was that everything possible had to be done to ensure a permanent destruction of the memory of Lobengula's kingdom. These plans included taking Lobengula's three sons to the Cape Colony under a pretext that they were to be educated. And one indeed might, in a cynical turn of mind, say there was good reason for that disposition among the white settlers because both Matabeleland and Mashonaland had from then on ceased to belong to the natives.

To the white settler there was no meeting point with the Matabele to bring about a spirit of reconciliation. One official of the Administration makes the point that after all the Matabele were usurpers. But the white people who also became usurpers did not come to Matabeleland because someone had destroyed their homes in England, whereas the Matabele were driven away from their homes in the Marico Valley in the Northern Cape by Dutch trekkers escaping British misrule in the Cape Colony. It was not greed or avarice that drove the Matabele from Kuruman to Matabeleland. It was a cruel necessity to find a new home for themselves.

Sojini and Hlazo, to return to our subject, were disappointed and this disappointment at the hands of a white lawyer led them to Alfred Mangena. Hlazo and his two sons Titus and Jeremiah were members of the 'Colonial Boys' at Mbembesi, with Hlazo an elected leader of the movement.

The Hlazo family became leading members of the Matabele National Home movement with Nyamande as its leader. This opened a great new world for Nyamande who had now moved from articulating personal grievances over land, to becoming leader of those calling for restoration of the Monarchy and its kingdom. He did not know what uphill problems he was to face; all these problems were created to erase all traces of his father's kingdom from the annals of history. That there was a formidable and race-slanted conspiracy to accomplish this goal cannot be denied. This plot embraced Lobengula's other children already in exile, as objects to be used to realize the goals of a bare-faced race-slanted consipiracy to achieve the objectives of an evil design, is also crystal clear.

Among the community of people at Mbembesi were teachers, nurses and clergymen recruited for Rhodes from Transkei by the famous 'Matabele' Thompson because Rhodes "was convinced of the usefulness of black settlers from South Africa that he took steps to bring up large numbers of them". One of the reasons for taking these steps was to solve "the native and labour problems of Rhodesia'. Their leaders and chiefs came to view the land that Rhodes had promised to secure for them before they returned to Transkei to bring up their families. They included six chiefs among them was Sojini. He and Hlazo later became aggrieved and bitter due to what they saw as Rhodes' unkept promises. But Rhodes had died in 1902 and the aggrieved men could no longer appeal to him to intervene or demand explanation. Rhodes successors simply treated their claims as presumptuous. Sojini and Hlazo became vociferous critics among those who had grievances against the Chartered Company.

As a punitive measure against the agitators the Company launched a squeezing out process to remove the people from their land which was then sold to white settlers, and Sojini and Hlazo were targeted for removal from their land. As the process of squeezing people from the land gained momentum, Sojini resorted to seeking recourse to law and intervention of the High Commissioner in Cape Town and that of the Aborigines Protection Society, without success and we see him resorting to leasing private land in Selukwe. We will see how the squeeze affected Hlazo in a shameful recital of betrayal on the part of the Chartered Company. We do not know how old Hlazo was when he and his people left the Transkei. We do know, however, that Hlazo was by 1916 aged 70 years when the Company moved to take the land from him after he had liquidated his debt to it.

Hlazo was a symbol of a fighter for his rights. He listed nine questions which the Native Commissioner failed to answer. He had been approached by a native policeman sent by the NC to ask him when he would be moving from one corner to another of his farm to make way for a white settler. He dismissed the policeman by simply telling him that he would be go in person to answer the question before the Native Commissioner. The nine questions make interesting reading. He listed the following questions to remind the Native Commissioner what happened to Adam at the Garden of Eden. The point he wanted to make was that Adam lost his tenure on the Garden of Eden because he broke God's Law.

In Hlazo's view the Chartered Company represented God in Mbembesi and had to apply the same principle that God applied to Adam at the beginning: You break the law then you are removed from the Garden of Eden. But if you keep the law you remain in the Garden of Eden which in Hlazo's view represented his land.

The following are the questions that stumped the Native Commissioner:

    1. Did we not fight for the Government in the Matabele Rebellion?

    2. Did the Government not give us a piece of ground as a reward for faithful services?

    3. Did the Government not give us a sketch or plan of the land for us?

    4. Did Government not say in his letter dated 15 November 1905, that the title will be issued to me after I had liquidated my debt? Has the debt not long since been paid?

    5. Have I not waited years for the title?

    6. Why did they not give the title after I had liquidated my debt?

    7. Was it because they wanted to take away again the land, they had given me?

    8. All these questions remain unanswered.

Hlazo's punchline in this drama of betrayal exposed on 17 December 1916 was admission by the Native Commissioner that Hlazo had not offended against the law. *"I have not had anything, and I searched all the records and I did not find a single crime that you did against the Government".*

Against this admission Hlazo retorted: *"I 'm an old man, over 70 years of age, and I was born under the British*

Government. *My crime must be very, very great, more than Adam's because the Government does not tell me what it is, all he says I must leave ...".* His crime was that he was an African. Africans, under the British colonial system, have no rights. We must assume that Hlazo went to his grave without title to his land which was passed on to white settlers and the people of Mbembesi continued to be squeezed out of their land until there was little land left for them to live happily. It is an incredible and sad testimony of what was happening all over Southern Rhodesia. The great land squeeze was on the move and legislation was instituted to give it legal face and respectability.

Under this legislation, white farmers with large settlements of Africans were taxed five shillings for every agreement with native "squatters" on their farms to force them to relocate to crowded Native Reserves in Matabeleland where soils are poor, and water is scarce. To make matters worse, Africans were not allowed to cross from one farm to another without a "pass" issued by the landowner. That the passes were often unobtainable created slave conditions on these farms.

On 10 March 1919 a gathering of interested personalities met at a house in Bulawayo's Makokoba location which belonged to a man named Malipe. Among the gathering was Nyamande's indomitable nephew Madhloli who once told a white farmer that he was free to kill him if he so felt. He was refusing to vacate a piece of land that had been his before it was sold to a white farmer, and Madhloli now rented it from the farmer. The farmer had decided to eject Madhloli from the land by refusing to accept his rentals.

Also present at the gathering was Titus, and so was Ngcayiya and others. Terence Ranger in his book *The African Voice in Southern Rhodesia (1970)* describes the petition that resulted from the gathering in the following words:

"Out of this meeting emerged a document which in some ways (was) a landmark in Rhodesian African political history, a petition to the King of England in the names of Nyamande and members of the family of the late King Lobengula and others of the Amandebele tribe in Matabeleland and Mashonaland ...' The AmaNdebele tribe in Mashonaland? What were they doing there?

Before proceeding with the main body of the petition, let me, in passing, warn the reader to be careful and avoid reading the preamble of the petition as expressing Nyamande's sovereignty over Mashonaland. And yet it does, and not without good reason. But if by argument it could be shown that the preamble claimed such sovereignty was unjustified, it could further be argued that the assertion was justifiable by looking at the historical circumstances to establish the true position in this regard.

It is common knowledge that Lobengula's sphere of influence before the Jameson Line of 1891 covered Mashonaland without the King claiming to be ruler of that territory. Moreover, the local chiefs did not challenge such sphere of influence. It is further common knowledge that the Mashona chiefs were not accountable to Lobengula and were not required to appear before Lobengula's Chiefs Council. But there is a further argument attached to the following question: Does history deny or recognize the fact that the Kingdom indeed included in its entity some 15 tribes a good number of whom were resident in Mashonaland, represented by such areas as Belingwe, Tshabane, Selukwe and Qwe Qwe? Can anyone deny that in fact the kingdom's sphere of influence extended to the Mozambique border before the Pioneer Column came?

An even more interesting question pertains to the failure by the people of Mashonaland to oppose the occupation of their territory, and their subsequent failure to articulate claims of the land they had been occupying, it has been claimed, for some 600 years, before Mzilikazi occupied Matabeleland. It is pertinent, therefore, to remind the reader that the legal team that was appointed by the Aborigines Protection Society to represent the natives at the land conference of 1919 represented the people of both Matabeleland and Mashonaland with Nyamande representing them as Petitioner. It was at this conference that the Privy Council granted the British Crown ownership of the land in both territories. Am I splitting hairs if I point out the fact that the people of Mashonaland had every right to send representatives if they so desired, but they chose not to do so? They were victims of occupation and alienation of their land as well as the Matabele. Moreover, they did not repudiate their inclusion in the preamble of the petition. And yet they chose not to protest.

It is a fact of life that Mzilikazi's appearance in Matabeleland was not challenged by anyone including the Mashona who are rulers over Matabeleland today. And the question remains: how did they come to wield so much power to assert their sovereignty over a territory they never conquered? The answer of course is that the British did that for them. There can therefore be no argument the Matabele kingdom was the only military power over Mashonaland before the white man came.

Let me remind those who have read my book, *The Rule by Conquest the Struggle in Mthwakazi (1915)* that I argue 'had the people of Mashonaland challenged Mzilikazi, they would have been driven back to Tanganyika or wherever they came from'.

The point is that Mzilikazi had the military power to drive them out but chose to co- habit with them as neighbours as long as they did not interfere with his settlement in Matabeleland and the Midlands.

The only military power that interfered with the established order of the kingdom was the Chartered Company supported by the Imperial Government and, for the first time in the history of the kingdom, the people of Mashonaland were there with the invaders to disturb law and order. But their presence in Matabeleland as rulers today is unsustainable because it thrives on tyranny and oppression like that which their white cooperating partners applied to the detriment of the African people. It is unsustainable because it was arranged by those whose grand plan was to drive a wedge between the people of Matabeleland and the Mashona in order to punish the Matabele. The foreign- inspired subjugation of the Matabele through the genocidal operations of the 1980s, coupled with the 2000 land reform programme which has been used to occupy Matabeleland, is fraught with grave danger. There is so much tribal tension between the Matabele and the Mashona because of what the British did in 1893 and continued in the 1980s in a coalition with the Mashona.

The perpetrators of the genocide may have escaped justice, but the people of Matabeleland are determined to become their own rulers. This is why it is so important that the government of Zimbabwe and the people of Matabeleland should start talks aimed at resolving the Matabele Question now. The United Kingdom, the British Commonwealth, Europe, the United States of America, supported by the United Nations, can help resolve the issue.

There is a crisis of identity among the people of Mashonaland who have sought to rely on mythology to establish the foundation of their identity. It is said a spirit medium foresaw the advent of 'kneeless people' (the white colonist wore pants that covered their knees down to their ankles) who would occupy the territory and later be driven away. The fact that the white man came with arms of war and was welcome for a while before being driven out 110 years later, makes the spirit medium's prediction credible but outside the realm of mythology, one would say.

But there is something missing: This is the fact that 52 years before the white man arrived, Mzilikazi occupied Matabeleland and found no Mashona in effective presence there. There was conveniently, also no Mashona spirit mediums in Matabeleland to predict his arrival or the fact that his warriors wore skin aprons and carried spears! But according to political rhetoric by the rulers of Zimbabwe, Matabeleland (the territory was then known as Mthwakazi) the territory Mzilikazi settled in to build a kingdom was under the control of the Mashona! This is the kind of adulterated history that spawns fanaticism.

Mashona historians are frightened to admit the fact that the Mashona involvement in the 1896-7 uprising was an accident of history which owes its reality to a man named Mukwati (Makwati) who led the uprising in Matabeleland when it broke out. He fought in the Battle of Intaba ZikaMambo in Matabeleland before going up north to start the uprising in Mashonaland.

The Mashona had no hand in planning the uprising. Being a Tonga captured at Monze in Zambia by the Matabele warriors', Mukwati was neither Shona nor Ndebele by tribe. It will be seen, therefore, that mythology is not an accurate yardstick with which to determine one's identity. It is nothing but a pack of wishful thinking and a contrived make-believe nonsense!

This is a long and emotive subject but for now let me pose a question: How does the reader understand the fact that the land grab by the British government affected both sides? This is in spite that there is nothing to show that the people of Mashonaland offered any protest against occupation of their own territory in the first place, and their failure to oppose recommendations of the Morris Carter Commission which closed the chapter on the land question for all time.

Is it unthinkable that, in their occupation of Mashonaland in 1890 the colonist, in a strategy to win the support of one of the two sides, deliberately played one against the other? The same cannot be said though about Mzilikazi whose policy was *Isizwe ka selukwe* (let the nation be knit together) from all the tribes, without distinction. From those he met on the way to Matabeleland to those he found in the land between Limpopo and the Zambezi.

Mzilikazi, a world-famous nation builder, felt that there was enough space for all to live together in peace. He had done the same among the Bakwena of the Northern Cape from where he was driven by Boers from the Cape Colony. But his policy has been under- mined by persistent and often hysterical proclamations that the Matabele are black settlers just like the white man and must, therefore, return 'home'. What about the lessons to be learnt from Zwangendaba who went through the Zambezi valley, reaching the south of Kenya before returning to settle in Nyasaland?

What about lessons that must be learnt from Mbuzeni (Mpezeni) who, ten years before Mzilikazi settled in Matabeleland, crossed the Zambezi to settle east of present-day Zambia? Furthermore, there is Soshangane who settled south-east of present-day Zimbabwe... Has the world ever heard the people of Malawi or Zambia complaining about the Nguni people in their respective countries as settlers to be pushed back to South Africa? Moreover, the Government of Zimbabwe is silent on the right of Soshangane's people to occupy the southeast of the country. So, what is the big fuss about Mzilikazi and his people settling in what became his Kingdom? It is noteworthy that the Ndau people of Gazaland have recently divorced themselves from the Shona bracket, but accepting that, for political reasons, they have all along been called Shona.

Before we return to the subject of the petition, let me observe that a question was raised as to the response of the people of Mashonaland and those of Matabeleland to the decision of the Privy Council of 1919 which rejected African claims on land that had been taken from them. On page 67 of Ranger's book, here is how he answers it:

> 'There was in fact little articulate response in Mashonaland, though the affected tribesmen who had to move out of the areas ceded to European occupation remembered it with bitterness for many years. But in Matabeleland a movement of protest on a wide scale began to develop. It was still the Ndebele who had the greatest grievance over land".

These sentiments are also expressed by the Superintendent of Natives following the Carter Commission of 1914. The Matabele people had already died in their thousands trying to stop invasion by a foreign power which was using an array of heavy weaponry and weapons of precision which won them the war against the Matabele.

I will deal at length with the subject of grievances as seen by the Superintendent of Natives in Bulawayo. But it is noteworthy that the affected tribesmen in Mashonaland merely remembered their deprivation with (mere) *bitterness* for many years! But then who has given them *legitimacy* to rule over Matabeleland with an iron rod?

It is the British Government, through the skulduggery of Margaret Thatcher's man in Rhodesia, Lord Christopher Soames, who gave Robert Mugabe the elections in 1980 after first considering the ban of ZANU for violent intimidation that affected voters in eastern districts of the country.

Admittedly, this is no longer an issue, but the British cannot say the Mugabe regime before 1980 created the problems that beset the people of Matabeleland today. These problems, history must recognize this, were deliberately created by the Chartered Company in connivance with the Imperial Government. This is not because the British liked the Patriotic Front better than Lobengula's children. The PF were simply used in a design to punish Lobengula's future successors for the crime of Lobengula's perfidy. And to imagine that the Mashona suffered in this manner when they had died supporting the British against the Matabele, boggles the mind.

There must be authority within the British system of governance to explain why the natives were treated in this shoddy manner. Can the British people still claim that their national conscience was not violated by a group of libertines out on the rampage to make money? To whom was the Company accountable? To its shareholders in London, Paris and Berlin who by remote control played the role of a dog in the manger while the rightful owners of the land became nomads moving from one farm to another of land held by absentee so-called owners.

I am writing this book for the record only so that coming generations can gain from it the knowledge of the march of history and the so-called advance of civilization in Africa that went terribly wrong.

The Crown in 1919 asserted that the land had become that of her Majesty's Government. Could this claim be justified under any law or authority in force anywhere in the world when peace treaties with the kingdom were flagrantly violated by the coalition of the United Kingdom and the British South Africa Company in a betrayal of Lobengula's trust?

I am raising this issue because it has been shown that both conquest and the concessions claim ed by the Crown as licence were not justifiable. This was more devastating to the Matabele than it was to the Mashona. And it is easy to explain why it had to be so. The Matabele in their tens of thousands had died fighting against the invaders and had to be penalized. This was despite the fact that relatively small numbers of the invaders lost their lives in the war.

The Matabele warriors did not, however, just accept that their land and cattle could just be lost to settlers because the invaders had machine guns. They demonstrated their discontent at the Lower Shangani encounter where they wiped out Allan Wilson's party, and later staged an uprising to overthrow the yoke of subjugation and brutal oppression which was to become the order of the day. What more could they be expected to do against such heavy odds? But their land and cattle were gone forever. We are told that Alan Wilson and his party stood at attention and sang their national anthem 'God Save Our Gracious Queen' who was about to sign those notorious Orders in Council to the detriment of Africans. I have no quarrel with loyalty, but I have a conscience to obey. But there was more to come years later when the Crown and the Company swapped places to prepare the ground to surrender the land to settlers without admitting they were doing so, with the Company now among those who were claiming ownership of the land for themselves. This was done through the decision of the Judicial Committee of the Privy Council of 1919 which was a victory for settlers who had not even taken part in the war against Lobengula. And they were not all of them British subjects. This was a scramble for African land while the scramblers left their homes intact in London, Paris and Berlin. This was a coalition of the Crown and allies across Europe.

By this process the British Government was shown to be in the market that dealt in contraband in the form of stolen native land and cattle to advance their flawed civilization. Persistent efforts, first by Lobengula and subsequently by his heirs to be admitted into the community of protectorates, were rudely rejected. Nyamande was told that if he If he persisted in his call for restoration of the monarchy and putting himself forward as his father's successor in a bid for a self-governing territory, he risked being sent to prison or being exiled like his brothers Njube, Nguboyejna and Mphezeni had been exiled to die in a foreign land, unknown and uncared for. When he persisted with his call, his freedom to live among his people was restricted.

CHAPTER 15

NYAMANDE'S EPIC LETTERS

THERE are two epic events in Nyamande's life that show that he was not just a warrior prince of little standing among the Matabele. The first one was his letters to the indunas in the territory circulated just about the same time as Ngcayiya tabled before King George V Nyamande's Petition on the land question and the Monarchy. The other epic event was his interview with the Administrator of Southern Rhodesia on which he was accompanied by leading monarchists in the former kingdom. During the interview it had been decided to allocate to him enough land for his personal needs within a Reserve in which the people had no security of tenure. But this attempt to buy him off went against his principle and desire and Nyamande rejected the offer.

This offer came just before the Administration discovered he was already circulating his epic letter among leading indunas in the territory.

The Administration had the letter translated, and that marked the beginning of the end for Nyamande, with the Administration removing him from his people to be restricted to his rural home.

It was after the discovery of these letters that the Chartered Company threatened to have him exiled and it was decided among his followers to have his nephew Madhloli as spokesman for the monarchists. It was Madhloli and the Weslayan teacher, Ntando, who led a delegation of 30 indunas to interview the High Commissioner in Cape Town where they were told in no uncertain terms to forget about their homeland enterprise. Nyamande could not join them because he had been refused permission, not only to visit his lawyer Ngcayiya in Pretoria, but also to table another Petition before King George in England.

We will see how as part of a strategy to frustrate him, Prince Arthur of Connaught as High Commissioner based in Cape Town, ordered Nyamande to return the money he had collected from his people to finance his travel to London.

In an interview with the Administrator, Nyamande asserted: "I suggest we follow the plan made by Mr. Rhodes". According to him the plan entailed the creation of two states within Matabeleland, one for Lobengula's people and the other for white settlers. Nyamande spoke with so much authority like one who was present at the peace indaba in the Matopos when Rhodes faced 28 leading indunas to negotiate peace during the 1896 uprising. He was certainly a leading figure in the uprising and was on the list of proscribed leaders of the uprising many of whom were tried and hanged for their role in the rising. He escaped the same fate through a general amnesty declared by the Chartered Company in December 1896.

One of those who attended the so-called Peace Indaba and was spokesman for the insurgents, was Induna Somabulane who told Rhodes that the Matabele were not to be treated like anyone's underdogs. The Matabele would rather die than to be treated like dogs. After Rhodes died the Administration simply denied the existence of such a plan.

Unkept promises also affected the Xhosa community in Mbembesi where leaders like Chief Garner Sojini and Ethiopianism leader, John Hlazo, who maintained that Rhodes had promised them secure tenure on land. But this is another subject whereby the Administration reneged on Rhodes's promises after his death.

To return to Rhodes's plan as stated by Nyamande, can any reader see leaders of the insurgents walking away from their meeting with Rhodes without any undertaking on his part that their land rights would be secured? After all it was the land question and of course the expropriated cattle that caused the uprising.

Back to Nyamande's interview with the Administrator of Southern Rhodesia:

It was held on 19 April 1920, and accompanying Nyamande were three uncles Joyi, Mbamba and Bidi, with one Haubasa also among them. Nyamande opened by outlining his two-states plan which would follow the watershed marked by the Cape to Cairo railway line which reached Bulawayo in 1902 just as Rhodes went to his grave.

This would mean that all the rivers flowing into the Zambezi fell within the parameters of Nyamande's homeland.

"My heart tells me that I should live in the country where my father's people were. I have asked my people for money to buy land". Said Nyamande.

He was aware that some of the land in his plan was already occupied (by whites). It was for the government to decide how he was to acquire it. He could not be any clearer. Then it was Joyi's turn.
Recorded below is parts of a transcript with the Administrator:

Joyi: "We are all contributing to the purchase of land: the whole nation is doing it. It is not Nyamande only.
The Administrator: "The question of so large a tract of

land is out of the question".

Nyamande: 'Then my only course is to go on (pushing) until I drop (dead).

The Administrator (retorting): "You have lived very well for the past twenty years as you are".

Nyamande had since January 1897 been restricted to his rural home to frustrate his influence pertaining to the homeland issue. The exchange went on with Nyamande saying all the problems the people were experiencing were caused by the influx of so many white people into the country.

His father's people were being pushed far away to suffer mosquito bites and to be eaten by wild animals.

The Administrator: "You are to understand that you have no responsibility for the wants of the people. You may speak for yourself and your own personal grievances. When your father was conquered, the requirements of his people became my responsibility", to which remark Nyamande responded: "Must I go and live alone in the forest"? (Nyamande in fact ended lived alone in the forest, rather than accepting the Administrator's offer of land for his personal needs.) He was told he had to accept the result of the war.

Joyi : "We are your children by right of conquest. Is it good policy for you to drive us away from you and not allow us to see you (to put our grievances before you)? Is it wise to drive your children away to the faraway parts of the country?

There is no record as to how the Administrator responded to Joyi's attack.

Then Haubasa bluntly charged: "You accept responsibility for the people belonging to the overcome king you must take care of the orphans".

But I think the punch line came from Bidi who

declared: "We as earnestly desire this tract of land as our nephew Nyamande. We don't want to be always troubling the Government. We are chased from farm to farm". This was a call for a homeland, for independence.

The meeting ended with the Administrator offering Nyamande land for his personal needs, which offer he rejected. The lesson to be learned from this interview is that it showed convincingly that Nyamande was indeed a popular leader for the Matabele National Home movement. He was prepared to sacrifice his personal comfort for the cause of his people. But the reader has not seen the climax of his life which is represented by the letters he wrote to leading chiefs in the former kingdom. With their discovery by the Administration, the beginning of the end for Nyamande was reached. This came with the translation of his letters to leading chiefs in the territory.

The letter is long but has an important message not to be ignored. It shows how Nyamande was undaunted in his quest for a national home for his people in the face of hostile frustration by the Chartered Company. This process bought for white rule 57 years more of relative peace before the winds of change caught up with them. The letters indeed reveal a rare talent in his expression of ideas.

"At the beginning I greet thee, my child" said a letter to induna Mafindo on 11 June 1919. *"Help me, Sitole by passing on those documents on that subject (the restoration of the monarchy). When your brother Sibindi was still existing, before his death, I sent a word to him as the child of a great induna and said that he was to repeat it to all izinduna of the nation. Well, I have not yet found his reply. Your word which I tell you ye children of izinduna of my house is this: You know that all tribes were overcome by the white men, but they have a place in which to remain happily.* [He was referring to the British protectorates in Southern Africa]. *It is only here in this country where the people remain unhappy. Well the other tribes*

paid money and they pay for their country where they sit down in happiness. We pay our money and sit down on farms (of white men).

As for me how do I come to speak of the country? I am unhappy ... Why is it that the paths that lead to me are overgrown with grass while you continue to pay each other visits over there? [The chiefs were not allowed to visit him in his restriction camp.] *I want your reply seeing that you are the head of the nation. The child that does not complain dies while working. Understand well men, I shall soon speak.* [There are two points from this statement to be noted: he was humbling himself before his elders a good many of whom belonged to his father's generation. The other point is that Nyamande was appealing to these elders to see him as a man ready to lead the nation for the general good].

Well men, what do you say? We remain in a scattered state all the time. Even if people have been conquered may they not abide in one place? For myself I ask of you, ye owners of the Territory in as much as ye are the nation.

I do not say it is war, my compatriots, I only inquire. You also know that all black tribes in great numbers were overcome by the white people, but they have their piece of land to stay on happily... We, forsooth, pay only for staying on white men's farms and for what reason?

Manyeba Khumalo, chief of Mzinyatini, I write this paper of mine to you all chiefs of the Regiments... I say to you all and the Sky Stabbers, I, Nyamande Lobengula Khumalo, whom you do not know, you Sky Stabbers all and your chiefs I do not see you, Oh People! I say to you all nations that have been conquered by the English the Government gave them Chiefs to whom they pay their tax. Look at Khama! He has his country, and Lewanika, he has his plot. His country is settled well, and Mosheshe, he has his land. Also, the son of Dinizulu has his country. All natives have their bit of ground where they pay their taxes. They pay their taxes they know and not like you who pay for what you know not.

You do not know what is done with your money .... At the same time you undergo tribulation.

Ntola Khumalo I say to you Big Chief of the Dynasty tell these other chiefs of yours, Khumalo, I have put in my word to the Big King,"Thunderer as he sits" , "Silence let us hear ", King George asking him what did father wrong to the Big Queen who never ends. This is where the matter is, with the King, I say tell me, our Sky Stabbers, if this that I am doing is not right you should tell me quickly if you do not agree. If you agree help me with "tickeys", people of my father because I require money from you so that I can essay the road to cross the ocean and go to the King over the Water in England and talk with King George. I say to you, Oh People! a child who does not cry out dies in labour. If you are happy in your present state let me know".

There are features in his letters that are remarkable. Nyamande was not spoiling for war. He was still hopeful his mission would succeed. These letters were being circulated as the lawyer Reed Ngcayiya tabled Nyamande's Petition before the British monarchy. It called for a homeland as enjoyed by other defeated kingdoms in Southern Africa. He wanted to follow up what was happening in England by taking a delegation of chiefs to talk to King George. Although the money was available from donations by his people Nyamande was refused permission to go to England. On the fact that he was not planning to wage war, let me say there are people in Matabeleland who are calling for dialogue with those concerned in order to reach an amicable resolution of the Matabele Question. These are civic organizations whose voice is being drowned in the din of indifference by the current rulers. They will not institute an honest truth and Reconciliation Commission to establish who did what during the Gukurahundi Genocide of the 1980s.

CHAPTER 16

SUPERINTEDENT OF NATIVES'S VIEW

AN interesting phenomenon in the Anglo-Matabele war saga was that, against all expectations, not all servants of the Company turned a blind eye to the harsh manner in which the people of Matabeleland and Nyamande in particular were being treated. This, at least, was the case before the discovery of Nyamande's letters to monarchist chiefs who represented the majority in the Kingdom. This is revealed in an astounding document from one senior official of the Chartered Company which was publicly acknowledged.

This aspect of the Matabele land issue deviates sharply from the official view and is a refreshing feature in the land saga as expressed by an official of the Company as shown in the following document. The writer of the document was, at the time, the Superintendent of Natives based in Bulawayo. It sheds light to the background of the thorny issue of a homeland for the Matabele as driven by Nyamande and other supporters of the idea. It reads:

The report and findings of the Southern Rhodesia Native Reserves Commission have been studied by the large number of people, official or otherwise, interested in the very important matter of Native settlement ... I wish to advance my own opinion that, through no fault (it would seem) of the Reserves Commission, the formerly dominant tribe of this territory, through whom the first titles to the Territory were secured by whites (first by concession and later through conquest) are of all tribes now in the worst position in respect of land. (The concessions *referred to in this case were granted to other interests before the Chartered Company. There was for one example the Baines Concession of 1876).*

"It is true they were usurpers displaced by our usurpation but is never the less an unfortunate fact that the premier native race whose organizing power and gift for government enabled them to impose their will on the minor tribes, and whose inherent character must inevitably establish their major influence for good or bad in the future development and happiness of our natives, should now suffer from an ever- increasing dissatisfaction with the provisions made for them in this regard. [The SN lamented the fact that within a few months following conquest all their valuable grazing and tilling land had ceased to be theirs].

'Their misfortune was in the first place their national predilection for the red and black loams which coincided with the so-called shale formation. The quarts reefs occur here and again coincide with pasturage which their judgment informed them was the best for their cattle. Within a few months of the European occupation practically the whole of their most valued region ceased to be their patrimony and passed into the private estate of individuals and the commercial property of companies. The whole of what the term "ngapakati kwe lizwe" (the amidst of the land) conveyed, became metamorphosed, although they did not realize it at first, into alien soil, and passed out of the direct control even of the Government".

The Government referred to above, of course, was still the Chartered Company although the land by decision of Privy Council now belonged to the British Crown. White settlers flocked into the country and became a powerful political bloc against the Company. In the transition to Responsible Government, it was the settlers who called the shots and land passed out of direct control of even the Government even as overall administrative authority was held by the Imperial Government. That authority was reduced further with the granting of self-government in 1923, and the reins of government passed, not to members of the Chartered Company, but to white settlers! What in real terms was the difference between white settlers and the Chartered Company? The Imperial Government pretended justice had been served.

However, an important point to remember is that the Imperial Government could have retained for itself the administration of native affairs as called for in the Nyamande Petition. Under these conditions the British Government would have been obligated to invite Lobengula's children and relatives to the Lancaster House Conference in 1979.

It is my argument that the rejection of Nyamande's Petition in 1919 was used to exclude Lobengula's children from the crucial independence negotiations to determine their political future. The British Government's argument that the PF nationalists should have raised the question of their participation is lame and unconvincing. The British Government deliberately excluded them because it did not want them to participate. The British Government had already rejected the call for a protectorate status as stipulated in the Petition.

The plight of the people of Matabeleland has worsened since these remarks of the Superintendent of Natives were made in 1919. Since 2000, the year of Land Reform in Zimbabwe, the government of Zimbabwe has resettled in Matabeleland in excess of four million people from Mashonaland and the process is continuing without allowing the people of Matabeleland to be resettled in any of the regions of Mashonaland. The equalizer element in nation building was absent from the resettlement exercise to allay fears that the exercise was merely a tactic to drive the Matabele across the Limpopo.

The government has used the land reform, as already stated, to advance its agenda of hegemony in the guise of land resettlement. The axis of tribalism in power in Zimbabwe has with the help of Britain and North Korea among others, become a military giant in the region to suppress Matabele aspirations for nationhood, with the possibility that the newly established Military University is already taping on North Korea's nuclear technology.

CHAPTER 17

PRINCE ARTHUR'S REBUFF

THIS pronouncement came after several attempts by Nyamande to persuade the Administration to change its mind and give effect to his proposals. His endeavours were of course rebuffed, although he remained undaunted; always believing, it seems that things would change for the better after his interview with the Administrator. Prince Arthur had just succeeded Lord Buxton as the Imperial High Commissioner to South Africa, and Nyamande saw the appointment of Queen Victoria's nephew as a good omen because the Queen was regarded by the Matabele as a friend and protector. It explains why, against the backdrop of hostile reception by the Administration over the years, Nyamande remained hopeful.

His expectations were, however, cruelly misplaced. What had in the meantime brought the worsening relations with the Company was a letter Nyamande wrote to leading chiefs, not only to consider joining in support of his enterprise but also to contribute money to fund the purchase of a vast swathe of land to establish a Matabele national home, as already stated, if such land could not be donated by the colonist usurper. Money was also required to pay for his projected visit to London, if necessary, to appeal to the King.

His appeal to the people of Matabeleland as revealed in the letter he wrote in his own language, received overwhelming support, causing a stir within the ranks of the Administration. Instead of going ahead with offering Nyamande adequate land of his own to appease him, the

Administration went full throttle to suppress his activities from there-on. Although he was still burning with the spirit of hope and determination, his interview with Prince Arthur proved to be the one that broke his dogged nature, leaving him to die a recluse, with a crushed spirit of hope he had not shown over the years.

Similar treatment had already been meted out to his brothers, Njube and Nguboyenja which culminated in their early death. The harassment of Njube and Nuboyenja finally, as we shall see, broke the link between the past and the future of the Matabele kingdom for the foreseeable future. The reader might be left wondering how he was able to pen a letter of this magnitude in his own language when (it is believed) he had never seen the inside of a classroom!

Professor Terence Ranger in his wonderful book *The African Voice in Southern Rhodesia (1970)* does not explain either. But let me hazard a guess. In 1859 King Mzilikazi and Dr. Robert Moffat, the father of John Moffat the author of the John Moffat Treaty of 1888, signed an agreement to build a school for boys which is known to this day as Inyati Boys School. Its curriculum was to teach Matabele boys building, carpentry, roadmaking and mining. This was 31 years before the Pioneer Column occupied Mashonaland. It is probable that Nyamande went to school at this institution and remained there long enough to learn how to write. Ranger's book states that Nyamande wrote the letter in his own language, and not that it was written for him.

The interview with Prince Arthur on 15 December 1920 opened with an address of welcome to the prince which was signed by Nyamande and his uncle Joyi and nephew Madhloli. The address was written on their behalf by none other than Rev. Msimanga of the Independent Methodist Church of South Africa and expressed loyalty of the Ndebele nation to the British monarchy. It was delivered by Nyamande himself and the following is its full content:

> *This appointment is an omen of good things and hailed by the whole of the Matabele tribe with great satisfaction and rejoicings because her late Majesty Queen Victoria was not only a Protector and Friend of subject races like ourselves but was the symbol of Justice and Right for all peoples. As a descendent of that High and Noble ruler, the Mandebele tribe regard Your Royal Highness appointment as a signal proof that the Imperial Government intends to live up to the ideals, traditions and policy of Your Royal Highness' Grandmother.*

Events had then moved toward a confrontation with Nyamande whose petition demanded a self-governing territory for the Matabele. On 23 October Connaught's reply was widely published in the Press to shatter Nyamande's dogged hopes once and for all.

In his reply, Prince Arthur refuted speculation among the ranks of Nyamande's people that he had given him encouragement to hope. The Prince's reaction was delivered in a tone bristling with Royal anger instead.

> *I will be patient and tell you once again that you are watched over carefully and you cannot now have another ruler besides the Government under which you live, to divide the rule of that Government, which has governed you wisely, to place it under a ruler of your choosing. You are prosperous and you and your families and increasing herds are not molested, and the King does not wish to go back from this pleasing state of things, even though you are **foolish** and ask it. The reserves are wide and fertile and are sufficient for the needs of the people for whom they are intended for very many years."* He continued, *'Africans who remained on European farms had chosen for themselves to experience conditions of life which must be different from what they would experience among their own people.* [The conditions

they experienced by 'choosing' to remain on white farms were the institution of slavery].

I may tell you that native interests are always watched over carefully by the King's Government'. [This was a direct threat against Nyamande for persisting to call for a homeland.]

The money Nyamande had collected from his people had caused the Prince "great displeasure and the money must be returned". "You are prosperous, and you and your increasing herds are not molested and yet you are foolish enough to ask for your own territory to govern yourself!" What royal racist arrogance to rattle another prince! This was the colonial despot's standard of treating dispossessed Africans. What right did the Imperial Government have to molest Africans when they protested about their land?

The 1914 Carter Commission had recommended that one million acres of good land be removed from the ambit of native reserves and Africans were expected to cheer. When racial snobbery and bigotry are extolled as virtue and legitimate aspirations of the conquered are suppressed by such utterances as were pronounced by Prince Arthur, this attitude must be condemned in the strongest possible terms.

Did Prince Arthur forget that the British Crown, according to the ruling of the Privy Council, succeeded Lobengula and that it was the British Crown that rendered the Matabele Kingdom defunct and, therefore, still held the power or authority to restore the kingdom to Lobengula's surviving children? What had happened to that authority in 1979 when the British Government passed the buck to Joshua Nkomo and Robert Mugabe as nationalists who should have raised the issue of a national home for the Matabele? What had happened to the Matabele nationalists themselves? They had been disarmed and their bid to rise again suppressed most cruelly to pave way for the likes of Mugabe and Nkomo. The Imperial Government, as king maker, prepared the ground long before the two so-called nationalists were born to make sure the Matabele Kingdom was vanquished for all time. That citation on the wall of the Bulawayo Cenotaph makes it abundantly clear the last thing the British people wanted to see was the resurgence of the Matabele Kingdom.

Briefly, one must record the fact that the adequacy and quality of land ceded to natives was poor, inadequate and was underscored by insecure tenure, but Prince Arthur pretended otherwise. We have seen how John Hlazo in Mbembesi, for one example, was treated.

This was bitterly criticized by missionaries like Shearley Cripps and John White who championed the native cause on the land. They pointed out as one example the imbalance in the Carter Land Commission's Report recommendation to reduce land held by natives by a whopping one million acres. This arrangement was accomplished through a complex land swap which left a debit balance of poor land to the natives.

Moreover, in official circles, as we have seen, the Superintendent of Natives was unwilling to support the views expressed by the Prince on the quality or adequacy of land held by Africans when implementation of the Commission's recommendations had been finalized for all time.

The SN's viewpoint had a positive effect on policy which is reflected by the Administrator's admission that land needs for the natives would have to be revisited to meet an expected growing need for their benefit. This admission was despite the finality of the land question as pronounced in the Carter Commission's recommendation. On the other hand, the Imperial Government laid down its policy in 1919.

This policy was that there was adequate provision for African needs as pronounced by Foreign Secretary, Lord Milner, who dismissed the Ngcayiya Petition on behalf of

Nyamande as totally without foundation. How does one explain the obvious disparity between the firm policy pronounced by Lord Milner and the opened-ended admission by the Administration in Southern Rhodesia that native land needs had to be considered? But there were ambiguities and inconsistencies in policy which worked against native interests. The matter gets even more difficult to understand when viewed against the failure by the Chartered Company to deal with the crowded settlements in Native Reserves. There was no intention on the side of both the Imperial Government and the Chartered Company to resolve the situation and move towards appeasing African grievances. Already there was increasing and determined calls by Nyamande and others for a protectorate for the Matabele which was met by a blunt rejection of the idea, and the two sides had become deadlocked, with the Matabele on the losing side.

This impasse was reached when Prince Arthur of Connaught on 23 October 1919 told Nyamande that the end had been reached in the land question.

"You are prosperous and you and your families and your increasing herds are not molested, and the King does not wish you to back away from this pleasant state of things, even though you are foolish and ask it", Prince Arthur told Nyamande.

But the reader must understand that the land issue and indeed the monarchy issue had nothing to do with justice. The land report, therefore, gave officials of the Chartered Company authority to simply ride roughshod over the natives, to give proof of their supremacy as a race. The welfare of the natives, their feelings, their happiness and indeed their self-esteem did not worry the Chartered Company. The African owners of the land were being treated like animals of the veld.

CHAPTER 18

NYAMANDE THE KING

AMID quibbling about Nyamande's right to succeed King Lobengula, there is all the evidence that he did become the third king of the Ndebele state in June 1896. The fact about his coronation is revealed in the thesis *Ndebeles Under the Khumalos 1820 – 1896* by Julian Raymond Dennis Cobbing which was submitted in May 1976 for the Degree of Doctor of Philosophy at the University of Lancaster.

According to the thesis, leading Ndebele chiefs met at Entumbane on 13 February 1896 to consider Nyamande's coronation as third king of the Ndebele kingdom. Following this meeting-in-council over which Dhliso Mathema presided, supported by Babayani Masuku and Sikombo Mguni, Nyamande's coronation followed on June 25 at the same venue. The man who introduced Nyamande to members of the Chief's Council was Mlugulu Khumalo who held the rank of Prime Minister that under Mzilikazi was held by Mncumbata.

Dismissing claims by the Chartered Company that the 1896 rising owed its place in history to the Mwari cult, Cobbing writes that "the Ndebele (were) led during the war of 1896 by the contemporary political hierarchy, but that for a short period of time the monarchy in the person of Nyamande was restored".

Cobbing records that, as the war came to an end "finally in December, Nyamande himself came in". His return to Bulawayo followed the proclamation of a general amnesty.

This followed the application of a scorched earth policy to starve the insurgents and their families to submission. This high-handed policy of attrition led to the so-called peace indabas that were held with leaders of what was known as the "Matopos rebels" among whose leadership was Somabulane who acted as spokesman for the 28 chiefs who faced Rhodes and his group. Apart from Nyanda, there was no other member of the royal family present at these so-called peace meetings. Cobbing says although reports of Nyamande being king were well known, no attempts were made to speak to him.

"On the contrary, such a course was ruled out because of possible future political difficulties", he writes. This marked the beginning of the Company's Native Department policy of "elevating minor leaders and reducing major leaders". It is common knowledge that those who were elevated came from the ranks of chiefs who had collaborated with the colonists during the rising. Six chiefs are named as having collaborated with the colonial government during the rising. It is a matter of historical record that Njube's and Nguboyenja's mothers, respectively, came from two of the six collaborating chiefs who are among the most leading in Matabeleland today.

Nyamande had surrendered in December after the amnesty and in January 1897 he was appointed senior chief for the district of Bulawayo and when he rejected his deposition to the level of a mere chief, he was restricted to his rural home of mid-Mbembesi area of Insuza. After that there is a total blackout about him or his movements and activities, until 1914 when we see him establishing contacts with leaders of the South African Native Congress.

The difficult political fears that were feared by the Chartered Company in 1897 did not simply go away with what in fact was a purging of the Matabele monarchy, as shown by Nyamande's continued articulation of the subject of restoration of the monarchy which peaked during the transition to responsible government which finally came in 1923.

There is a rider to be added to the monarchy and the homeland issue: it is that there was no peace treaty or armistice as a result of Rhodes' meeting with 28 chiefs in the Matopos. The warriors did not surrender their weapons. What brought an end to the rising was the destruction of food reserves and livestock wherever these could be found, which resulted in people being starved into abject surrender. What, therefore, became critical in the campaign to suppress the rising was the application of the policy of the thin end of the wedge which was applied by the commander of the British Imperial forces Frederick Carrington. The suppression of the rising had become a coalition of Imperial forces and those of the British South Africa Company. This brought about a general surrender of the entire population and was followed by an amnesty which saw Nyamande returning to Bulawayo where he was deposed and later restricted to his country home.

Can anyone call Rhodes' talks with only 28 chiefs in the Matopos sector of the war a peace treaty? If it is by any description a peace treaty or anything near it, why then were Lobengula's children and their supporters excluded from the Lancaster House talks? The only answer is that their inclusion would have negated the designs to purge the Matabele monarchy for all time. But is their exclusion from the Lancaster House talks a proof or not of the British Government's success in its designs to purge the Matabele monarchy? The Matopos talks with Rhodes did not result in a peace treaty or armistice with Great Britain. It was not even a truce. Are the people of Matabeleland, who survived extermination by this coalition, still in a perpetual state of war with Great Britain? The answer is an emphatic yes! Great Britain owes the people of Matabeleland an explanation as to why she surrendered their kingdom to the people's perpetual enemies without talking to them. What was Great Britain's grand design in surrendering Matabeleland to the people's enemy? The so-called nationalists joined the British Government in a coalition to deny the people of Matabeleland protection at the Lancaster House Conference.

This point cannot be over-emphasised. The British government cannot absolve itself by passing the buck to its allies.

It has been suggested that the Chartered Company's taking Njube and Nguboyenja into exile is an indication that the two young princes were more qualified to become king than Nyamande was. There is no credible evidence to back up this claim.

The critical historical fact is that the chiefs' council acted in accordance with the wishes of King Lobengula when they crowned Nyamande king to succeed his father. But neither of the three of them, as already stated, was favoured to become king. How could one or the others be favoured when the fundamental policy of the Imperial Government was to purge the Matabele monarchy?

Is Njube not the same man who was deported from Bechuanalabd back to the Cape Colony when he tried to return home without permission? His death followed within a year. How can anyone suggest one or the other of the three princes was favoured by the Chartered Company to succeed Lobengula? A critical point to remember is that those who are opposed to the lineage of Nyamande to produce a king are seeking a deposition of his lineage from which a new king must be found. While one of opponents of this lineage claims to represent Njube's, no evidence has been advanced why Nyamande's lineage must be disqualified. The third contestant comes from Hlangabeza's house. No reason has been advanced why someone from Lobengula's brother should qualify to be king ahead of those from the house of Lobengula. There is, moreover, irrefutable evidence that the Njube line is backed by elements outside Lobengula's house. Furthermore, among those who are opposed to Nyamande's line are chiefs from those who were elevated by the Chartered Company to oppose Nyamande. This has all the hallmarks of those who opposed Lobengula but supported Nkulumane. This is an attempt to perpetuate conflict that led to the civil war that preceded Lobengula's coronation in 1870.

CHAPTER 19

RHODES THE DESPOT

IN focusing attention on Njube, Nguboyenja and Nyamande, I have relied almost entirely on Prof. Terence Ranger's well-documented book *The African Voice in Southern Rhodesia. (1970)*. The book gives a better insight into their treatment than any other that might have been written about them. But even then, the author appears to have suppressed a great deal of what was available to shed more light on their life under Cecil John Rhodes and, after his death, the Chartered Company. This is to be regretted because the life of Lobengula's children is a subject of profound interest to the people of Matabeleland. This is especially true when it is remembered that Njube, Mpezeni and Nguboyenja were taken away purportedly to be educated. Numerous questions cross one's mind when it is realised that they never went further in that education but ended as just other natives. This raises a great deal of suspicion as to whether indeed their removal from their own people was not a design to frustrate them so that they did not grow up to become a threat to the Chartered Company as a result of their purported education. The motive to frustrate them in their quest for education is indeed overwhelming. Their removal from their people looms large as a great purge of the Matabele monarchy.

They were hounded, harassed, threatened and not allowed to live normal lives. This was despite the professed goodwill toward them which was seemingly manifested by Cecil John Rhodes' interest in their welfare. The Matabele nation was, therefore, robbed of a promising and far-reaching good that could have resulted from their contribution to society. Since Nguboyenja wanted to read for the Bar, can the reader imagine what impact his qualification would have brought to Matabeleland whose people remain the least educated in the country? He was poised to qualify as a barrister 50 years before the first African lawyer Herbert Chitepo qualified to practise law in Southern Rhodesia.

After reading accounts of their treatment by their professed benefactors, one is still left wondering whether Ranger told all he knew or suspected about the Company's treatment of the two princes after Mpezeni's drowning in Port Elizabeth on arrival in 1898. Ranger says for instance, that Njube was proving to be difficult in his relations with Rhodes. He wanted to return home. As an answer to his increasing nonconformist attitude someone close to Rhodes suggested that he should "quietly get rid of him". This must have been an official of the Chartered Company in Matabeleland writing to Rhodes in the Cape Colony.

Ranger's source is unnamed, and his curiosity was apparently not aroused. Was Ranger involved in a cover up? I think he was, and I will show how. There is, according to him, incontestable evidence that Cecil John Rhodes and others unknown, conspired to destabilize the lives of Lobengula's two sons. This led to their premature death. It is clear; therefore, they were taken away from home "to be educated" under false pretences. Moreover, Rhodes and the Chartered Company had the motive to suppress emancipation of Lobengula's children because their success would lead to all manner of problems for his establishment in Matabeleland.

Rhodes himself was a self-proclaimed despot who believed that despotism had worked so well in countries like India and had to be applied against natives in South Africa. He did not, by his own admission, believe in granting Africans the vote, so how could he take the two native princes to be educated so that they challenge the reasonableness of his philosophy? Does a despot care about the wellbeing or life of other people, especially those whose father was responsible for so much trouble for him in his colonial enterprises? He was once reported as proposing "equal pay for all civilized men" or words of that meaning.

In Rhodes' dictum or vocabulary, therefore, Njube and Nguboyenja did not measure up to the level of civilized men and should not be allowed to do so. They had to be cocooned into the level to which all Africans must, by the dictates of despotism, belong. He was no philanthropist by any standard and how could he invest in the future of children of his colonial opponent?

Born six months apart in 1853, Rhodes and Jameson attained university education with the illustrious Leander Starr Jameson graduating with a doctorates of Medicine to become the hatchet man of the Chartered Company, with Rhodes holding the purse strings. The point I want to make is that both had enough education to have been refined by it. But it appears there was no crime, as has been said, heinous enough for them to commit. There was no limit to the weapons they used to slaughter Africans. Jameson rushed into where the angels feared to tread.

Admittedly, the English phrase to get rid of something or someone is a metaphor – a figure of speech which does not necessarily mean to kill or to induce death.

But in this regard, it can be argued that the Chartered Company's treatment of the two princes induced a decline in their health which led to their premature deaths. This can be blamed on their purported benefactors' behaviour. It is outrageous because it leads to one conclusion which is that there was a conspiracy to cause instability in their health leading to their deaths. The design could only be to ensure they did not grow up to become a threat to the

Chartered Company.

Moreover, it is too much of a coincidence that of their male children after them, born in exile where they must have been hounded and denied freedom like their fathers before them, never made it in life either. But it should be left to the observer to perceive the extent to which their failure in life owed its force.

It is difficult for one to resist the conclusion that their removal from their people was a purge designed to ensure they did not make it in life, let alone be left free to choose the course of their future. This had everything to do with the political future of the Matabele Kingdom.

There was, moreover, a great deal at stake should the princes be allowed to develop their full potential and return home to create problems for the Chartered Company. This conclusion is strengthened by the fact that they were denied freedom of movement and choice and had to ask for permission every time they wanted to visit their relatives and friends at home. They were not conscripts in an army barracks. Why did they have to submit to this kind of injunction?

The only problems that could prove undesirable related to Njube's returning home to lead a rebellion against the Company. This applied equally to Nguboyenja and their treatment was, if you like, a carbon copy.

It can, therefore, be said that the Company in the circumstances decided to forestall the potential danger by issuing destabilizing injunctions against the two princes, with disastrous results for both. If the Company wanted the world to see their removal from their home environment as purely an act of benevolence in the princes' best interest, it failed dismally.

Did Rhodes or someone acting on his behalf cause Njube's and Nguboyenja's untimely death in 1910, hardly 12 years after being taken with their other brother Mpezeni to the Cape Colony to be "educated?" That conclusion, according to Terence Ranger, cannot be avoided.

Njube does not appear to have done well at school, and after being refused permission to return home, he became a disillusioned farmer in the Eastern Cape. We will see that the welter of destabilizing injunctions included the use of a neighbouring country to deport Njube back to the Cape Colony on extremely questionable and unconvincing grounds. After Rhodes' death in 1902, Njube became increasingly defiant of authority in his endeavour to be allowed to return home to his own people. His mother, Mpoliyana appears to have, perhaps unwittingly, tragically added in no small measure to his frustration.

Ranger appears to have cultivated good working relations with officials of the Chartered Company or those who apparently had information and allowed him access to confidential files about Njube's life.

It is perhaps natural that he was obliged to obey the ethical rules to protect a source of information. But he might have realized that by quoting information from these files, even though he did not name the source, this was bound to raise more questions than providing answers. Njube and Nguboyenja were no ordinary Matabele siblings. Their place in society was unavoidably on a high public plane and attempts to eclipse their profile by treating them 'like all natives" was bound to arouse suspicion.

In 1898 Njube and his two brothers were taken away from their people to be 'educated' in the Cape Colony.

No one seems to know how old they were but Mpezeni drowned that same year. The circumstances of his drowning are unknown. Njube and Nguboyenja did enter schools in the Colony somewhere, it appears, and Nguboyenja proved to be "academically cleverer" than his elder brother. He wanted to read for the Bar but was persistently and paternalistically discouraged by his purported benefactors.

It is not clear, however, if this came from Rhodes himself or officials of his Administration working under his direction or instruction. But it is clear that the officials could not have defied Rhodes' wishes if he wanted the young princes to be left alone to pursue without interference careers of their own choice.

After all, Rhodes' motive in taking them away from their people was seen as an act of benevolence or goodwill. After a great deal of argument with Company officials however, Nguboyenja won and was in 1907 sent to England to pursue his studies, only to return home in Matabeleland by 1908, a short eight months later. His stay in England is pretty murky but there can be no doubt that his health problem appears to have worsened while he was there. With Rhodes now dead, no explanation was forthcoming from the Company concerning the cause of his declining health. But it is clear that he and the Chartered Company did not agree on what course in his education he was to pursue. It is also common knowledge that his going to England had been forced on the Company by fears that his cause might attract undesirable attention in the public domain. So, the Company reluctantly allowed him to go England "for special training" which turned out to be something other than law.

There is nothing to give an insight into the cause of his depression problem when, it is known, he was bubbling, with good health and enthusiasm to study law and return to the Cape Colony to practise. On the other hand, it appears that the Chartered Company wanted him to be brought up 'knowing' his place as just another native. This will be shown in his interviews with officials of the Company.

It is not clear if he indeed entered college in England or was simply assigned a tutor. But his depression deepened, and this forced his early return home. There is room for speculation here because, in the absence of official explanation, no reason has been advanced or is known for his sudden unhappiness while he lived in England. Did the Administration deny him certain privileges because of his defiance and refusal to pursue what had been planned for him, to further a design to ensure he grew up knowing his place in society? And what were the fundamental reasons for their choosing a career for him? We shall look at Njube's case in due course but for now let us stay with Nguboyenja.

We have seen that in 1907 he was sent to England by the Company 'for further training". 'The Company idea was for him to become a Veterinary Surgeon. On the other hand, Nguboyenja was unyielding in his pursuit of a career as a lawyer. "Lobengula is essentially a student", his tutor reported, "and therefore the career of a veterinary surgeon does not appeal to him". The mention of a tutor is evidence enough that he did commence some trumped course of study. But it was not what he had gone to England to study and this caused a sharp decline in his mental health which was to lead to his death.

In a letter written to the Administration from England with a tone of anger he said, "I thought I had made it quite clear that it was the Law I would be taking on coming up here". In the meantime, the Company Secretary was "disturbed at the prospect". And he wrote: "I told Mr. Hibbert that, while no doubt a university education might be very desirable, I thought in the case of Lobengula it was scarcely necessary", he wrote without elaborating. Scarcely necessary? Company Secretary Inskipp himself interviewed Nguboyenja: "He told me he was very keen on becoming a barrister...". Nguboyenja, however, was told that time was not yet ripe for "members of the coloured races in South Africa to take up the learned professions as they then do in India and other parts of the world". "Did Nguboyenja wish to practise his profession in West Africa or other parts of the world?" Inskipp asked him.

Nguboyenja was still in England and it appears the matter was discussed in South Africa and a decision to force his return taken.

By the way, the assertion that Africans in South Africa were not yet ready to practice law in their own country was a mere claim without any foundation because Alfred Mangena had been practicing law in his native South Africa since 1912 or earlier.

If what appears to be a desire to force him to abandon his pursuit to study law was taken and force his return to the Colony is indeed true, was this achieved by denying him his allowances or something? The world shall never know. There was, moreover, the danger that his case might attract the attention of sympathisers in England which could prove embarrassing to the Chartered Company.

Ranger makes a terse but all the same interesting observation about Nguboyenja's ambitions. 'The prospect of a son of Lobengula qualifying as a barrister some half a century before Herbert Chitepo, who was to be in fact the first African lawyer in Rhodesia, is a tantalizing one". This observation of course was made with Ranger's tongue-in-cheek, to explain why the prospect was tantalizing.

But let me assure the reader that had Rhodes not driven away 600 000 head of Lobengula's cattle to be sold in Kimberley after the end of war in 1893 to finance the construction of the railway line which reached Bulawayo in 1902, Inyati Boys School in Matabeleland, founded by Dr. Robert Moffat in 1859 to teach Matabele boys carpentry, building, mining and road-making, as already indicated, might have become a centre of higher learning long before Chitepo was born to go to Fort Hare University in the Cape Colony to study law. The irony of it, of course, is that Chitepo was not Lobengula's son (or tribe) and did not suffer humiliation of being groomed to know his place as a native. This perhaps explains why Chitepo succeeded where Nguboyenja failed.

All the stops were being pulled out by the Administration to break Nguboyenja's spirits. On 31 July 1908 he wrote the following moving letter to Secretary Inskipp:

I am sorry to disappoint you and those concerned with my welfare so soon, by asking you whether it would not be possible for you to send me back home as soon as possible. I really cannot stay here any longer. I have tried my very best in fact I thought a change might improve matters.

But as it is I am no happier nor likely to be....This letter is the result of no hasty conclusion and I should be much obliged if you took it as such, for as to whether I could stay here any longer is a question that I have thought many a day and night. I know this letter coming so soon after giving you my word that I would help your endeavours on my behalf by doing my best to work hard and get through the Law course, will no doubt grieve you.

But I do not see how I can pull through in my present state. Every day is more gloomy than that before it.

He does not say what was bugging him and yet there is a discernible decline in his spirits. Why?

He was allowed to leave England for Matabeleland where he remained for only three months before he was whisked away back to the Colony to die.

The poor man was in prison. But if depression, as has been said, was the root cause of the state of his mind, why did the Company fail to take him to a doctor to be interviewed and examined to determine the real cause of his problem? The Company was obliged if for no other reason than that he was their ward, to do so. If they did, this information has been concealed from the public domain. Is it because it might have proved damaging to the image of the Company? Worse still was to come when he finally left England and returned home in Matabeleland.

And I might be allowed to observe in passing that his harassment was to prove to be a replica of that which Njube was soon to experience. Was there a plan to destabilize him as well?

It is said the Chartered Company authorities feared Nguboyenja much less than they feared Njube while he was still alive. But the harassment and humiliation that the Administration meted out against Nguboyenja were designed to destroy any attempt on his part to get close to those who were known to be working to have the Monarchy restored. It will be shown that, once back in Matabeleland, Nguboyenja proved to be a centre of attraction for his people from all walks of life and the state of his health improved noticeably. This was to prove to be his undoing as injunction upon injunction were placed against his freedom to work with his people for their general good. Back home in Matabeleland his first interview with the Chief Native Commissioner is extremely interesting, showing as it does that morbid paternalism was to be used to put Nguboyenja where all natives belonged.

CNC: *"You know, Nguboyenja, you are a child still and sometimes it is better to have someone to think for you."*

Nguboyenja was defiant and retorted: *"I think I am old enough to think for myself."*

CNC: *"I represent the Government and you must try to please me so that we can get on well together, you understand? All the black people know that I am in charge ... as long as they do what I tell them they are alright. I attend to their wants and you are in the same position ... We must be good friends otherwise there will be trouble. I am good friends with all my chiefs".*

What Nguboyenja wanted was to be left alone to

organize his life to lead his people to freedom, and that was not forthcoming from the Company. Nguboyenja was far from submitting. He wanted land and declared:

"There is any amount of wasteland in this country". As far as he was concerned, he had come home to stay. He did not see how Government could suffer loss of money, he said, by granting him what he was asking. He wanted to live among his people.

His presence among the people was attracting a lot of attention and their support surged, with veterans of the 1896 uprising like old Mlugulu defying standing orders from the District Commissioner to seek permission before visiting him. In what appeared to be a remarkable recovery from depression, Nguboyenja showed increasing interest in the welfare of his people in the Reserves. He went out of his way to ask for maps to establish the extent and location of these reserves.

In short, he became a thorn in the flesh of the Administration and had to be reined in to prevent his becoming a rallying figure to oppose the manner in which his people had, by definition, become slaves.

While all this was allowed to persist, the Chief Native Commissioner was moved to remark before a gathering of chiefs on 16 September 1908: 'There is a path he has to tread and that is the straight path which means he has to do all that I tell him ... if he misbehaves and there is the slightest attempt to kick against the Government in any one direction I shall take no responsibility and he shall not be allowed to remain in the country.

He is a native of this country and he must obey all the laws appertaining to natives," said the CNC. The cat was out of the bag! In the scheme of things was that Nguboyenja must play ball with the masters of tyranny on both sides of the Company's world in the Colony and in Rhodesia or take what was coming to him.

That was the end of the road for Nguboyena, from England to Cape Colony to Rhodesia, and back to Cape Colony where he died. His age when he died is unknown.

With his death, attention swung to Njube now living his last days in the Cape Colony to where he had been returned after being deported from Bechuanaland – at the request of the Chartered Company – when he tried to return home without permission of the Company.

With Nguboyenja back in the Colony a recluse talking to himself, a faction of the 1896 veterans of the uprising led by their commander Mlugulu, calls for Njube's return increased alarmingly by the day as the people from all walks of life joined in a popular demand for Njube's return, but the Administration was unmoved. They held the knobkerrie, as the Ndebele say, by its head. They held the trump card that would ensure that Njube remained exiled, to prevent further calls for restoration of the monarchy.

The only sections of the population who were conspicuous by their absence among the monarchists were a few loyalist chiefs who feared that Njube's return would deprive them of their large herds of cattle which the Administration had returned to them after their expropriation in terms of the 1894 Matabeleland Order in Council. We have seen that of the 41 000 herd of cattle that remained after the expropriation Order of December 1894, some cattle were returned to loyalist chiefs to be used in a strategy to drive a wedge between Lobengula's children and the generality of the people on one side and the loyalist chiefs on the other. We have already seen how this strategy was used against Nyamande who was to become a focal point among those who wanted restoration of the monarchy.

This approach by the Administration was designed to ridicule and humiliate Nyamande while loyalist chiefs lived in affluence from cattle that traditionally were held by the King for the people. And the Chartered Company, in an endeavour to obliterate any link or identity with Lobengula's past glory, the Company was now doling out the king's cattle to loyalist chiefs to destroy the Matabele heritage. This strategy was designed to erase all traces linking the present and the past. This, in my view, was the grand plan or motive behind Cecil John Rhodes to accomplish his mission when he took Lobengula's children away to be humiliated. The danger posed by their presence in the environment of Matabeleland was so hugely potent and threatening that it could not be left to chance to deal with it. And there was no other way of fixing it other than by taking them away, purportedly to give them a chance to advance in life. But the real motive was to remove them from a society in which dangers of insurrection lurked in the dark of the Matabeleland environment.

CHAPTER 20

THE NJUBE DEBACLE

SIGNS that Njube was unhappy surfaced in July 1908 when he wrote a pathetic letter to Inskipp asking to be allowed to visit home. Since information concerning his birth is unknown his age cannot be determined. But we know that he had been living away from home and friends for some 10 years. We also know that his mother had visited him in Cape Town at least once. But there was no escaping the fact that he was no longer the boy we saw writing Rhodes a letter asking his 'benefactor' to allow him to visit home. He felt it was time to go home for a while and meet old friends, and also get a few things attended to while he was there.

It is also probable that he was already thinking of getting married because one of the things he wanted done was having his own house in the same place where his mother lived.

His mother, however, was not ready to allow this at this stage, complaining to Njube that he was being misled by friends and reminding him of his promise that he would listen only to Rhodes whom, she said, was Njube's "only father". This might have been so while Rhodes was alive but Njube must have wondered what would happen to him when Rhodes died, and now he had been dead for six years and Njube wanted to emerge as a man on his own.

But before we see what was to happen to him, let us look at one schoolboy-like letter of appeal to Rhodes in October 1898. This apparently is one letter that has survived the passage of time. That it is the only one to survive is a tragic loss. He wrote:

My dearest Master. Please Sir will you let me go Home just for Holiday only. I will not ask you any when I have been Home. Please Sir I will not ask you anymore when I have been Home. Will you please have mercy on me. Please Sir I tell you do not think that I will rebel against you.

How can I do wicked things against because you are so kind to me, and you have to be so careful to me, and giving me what I want. You can tell me how many days or weeks I may stay at Home ... Please Sir have mercy on me that I may go and see my friend at Home, and I will come back as soon as you want me to come back. And I want to seek for some business and if I see that I can't have anything to do there I will come back again as soon as you want me to come back'.

The Company Administration was unwilling to allow him to return. It was then that 'one of Rhodes' correspondents urged him to "get rid of Njube quietly since there will always be trouble so long as he was alive".

We know now that there was indeed a plot hatched to terminate his life. What we do not know is what form the plan was to take. Was poisoning him to induce slow death one of the options considered? And was this method to be used against Nguboyenja? Before I focus again on Njube, let us take a look at his mother. She had visited Njube in the Cape at least once before Rhodes died, and she had managed to extract a promise from Njube that he would always consider Rhodes as his only 'father' to be always obeyed.

In April 1899 a young Induna, Somaxhegwana had visited Njube in Cape Town and on returning home, Njube asked him to tell Karl Khumalo (Lobengula's former secretary) to organize the building of a kraal for Njube 'Lobengula's principal son'.

Those who spread the word about this development

were prominent members of the veteran rebel group. Word got around to Mpoliyana who was not amused by these developments and she wrote a letter rebuking him. Whether she was driven by sheer self-interest or fear that Njube was still too young to get involved in national affairs, is anyone's guess.

"Rumours are about", she wrote to him, *"that you have ordered a kraal to be built for you by Somaxhegwana, son of Mzilane, and others. I wish to know at once if you did order the building of this kraal. My heart is very sore to hear these rumours about you.*
When I visited you in Cape Town you faithfully promised to do so. Do you believe people misleading you? My son, cling to Mr. Rhodes. He is your only father and guardian".

An unavoidable question is: Who was to be Njube's so-called father and guardian when Rhodes died, and his death came less than three years later. But it can be observed that Mpoliyana, who benefitted from a pension as Lobengula's widow, was driven by self-interest. She did not want her son to be involved in another conflict with the Chartered Company. But a pension for her or anyone else was not among Njube's concerns, and we see him progressively becoming defiant. This is reflected in his reply to his mother.

It may have passed the reader's notice that the polished language and tone of the letter show that it must have been drafted for Mpoyiyana by an officer of the Administration. In August of the same year Njube sent back an angry reply.

I received your letter alright. It is clear you do not wish me to return home. I wish to know what you want from me. Perhaps it is because you don't care about me anymore. I was under the impression that you do not care about me any longer since you drove away Mapitsholo who came to your kraal to erect me a house. Now you intend to drive away Somaxhegwana.

What do you wish me to do? I must wish you all good-bye. I will not come home again even if you reply to this letter, you better understand that I shall not return to my home". [Not if the Company had a say in it!].

But Njube did return home in 1900 when the Administration backed down and allowed him to visit home. This was to be his last visit.

There are several features to be observed from Njube's letter. Most important of these is the discernible improvement in his letters, showing that he had become mature and better able to communicate. It is also clear that he was no longer the pathetic servant in Rhodes' household.

There is a whole story to be told about Lobengula's family, his wives and children. The burning question is about them is: How did the Chartered Company treat them? Moreover, there is the story of Njube's children, Rhodes and Albert. Little is known about them, although Albert is buried next to Mzilikazi at Entumbane, a sprinting distance from Rhodes' grave at the World's View. It is important to establish the facts because they became "orphans" of the Company after Lobengula's forced flight into exile in a far-away land. Did they receive from their foster parents, the Chartered Company, the kind of treatment expected for their well-being?

Njube's visit caused a stir as friends and foe, anxious to satisfy their curiosity, flocked to see him. Leading among friends was Mlugulu who, like in the case of Nguboyenja, defied red tape imposed by the District Commission against those who intended to visit Njube. The DC declared Mlugulu's behaviour as remarkable conduct deserving punishment. "Mlugulu knows well that he has no right to leave the district without informing me", he was reported to have asserted.

There was a general agreement among leading chiefs, teachers and the educated that Njube should return home to lead them. The Administration, however, was getting worried and in 1903, to put an end to agitation, acted swiftly and Njube was taken back to the Cape Colony amid pronouncements that he would not be allowed to return. But the drama surrounding him was still to be played out.

With Rhodes now dead, Njube was no longer submissive. He continued to send messages to his supporters in Matabeleland and in 1904 he forced the issue of his return by writing a letter informing the Administration in Matabeleland that he was returning home without their permission. The Administration moved swiftly, requesting the High Commissioner in Bechuanaland to issue a warrant authorizing Bechuanaland Police to arrest and deport him back to the Cape Colony.

And that marked the end of the Njube saga, with his death coming in 1910.

Before we close the chapter on Njube, let us look at developments back home which were characterized by increasing demands for his return and how the Administration reacted to them. Nothing sums up the unyielding mood of the Administration better than the following pronouncement by the Administrator before a gathering of Matabele chiefs:

'They (the chiefs) have said to me again and again that there is one thing they particularly desire, but they must learn to know me. When I say No, I mean No. The son of Lobengula is well and being well looked after in Cape Colony, *but he is not coming back here*' declared the Administrator to another official of the Company. The purging of the Matabele monarchy was getting tighter. Was there a fear within the Administration that his return might prove the Administrator wrong in his claim that Njube was "well and being well looked after"? This pronouncement was delivered before a gathering of Matabele chiefs and was widely publicized in the country and abroad. On 25 November 1909, Njube wrote angrily to the High Commissioner a letter that proved his last. He died seven months later. The strain of being hounded from his home was simply unbearable.

This is the text of that letter:

I observe from reports of His Excellency's speech in Rhodesia that I am not to be allowed to return to my country. What the cause of this decision maybe I know not and can assume it is a fresh "Colour Bar" on the eve of Union ...

I am a peaceable man who has done no harm to my king and country, and yet I am hounded from my own home while Members of Parliament in England like Mr. Victor Grayson, and Mr. Keir Hardie, Mr. Lloyd George and Mr. Winston Churchill, all publicly avowed anti-monarchists and consequently, I assume, rebels, are permitted to continue their propaganda unmolested.

What was the degree of molestation the Matabele princes suffered?

Njube was no longer the schoolboy who wrote that letter to Rhodes in 1898 asking for permission to visit his home. He was now a mature man who valued his freedom to act according to the dictates of his mind. It was this maturity that won the day among monarchists but was seen by the Administration as a threat to the Company.

The High Commissioner responded to the letter by remarking that the letter was one "that will require to be carefully answered" but death robbed him of that opportunity as Njube conveniently died before the High

Commissioner had had time to respond.

It will be recalled that before the chapter closed on Njube and Nguboyenja, and the pendulum swung to focus on one surviving son of Lobengula, Nyamande, the Administration did not let up on their drive to destroy any memories of the kingdom. Was it a coincidence that Nyamande also died, not only as a result of morbid depression but also as a recluse? I will leave that to the reader to judge.

I have argued in this book that civilization as one presented reason for the Chartered Company's invasion of Matabeleland was tragically flawed. The Company's unrelenting hounding of Lobengula's children vindicates that argument.

The people of Matabeleland may have lost a kingdom but civilization – by way of the haunting injunctions suffered by Lobengula's children – lost all credibility and became nothing but a sham.

Let me illustrate my point by telling an amazing story of criminal immorality in which an official of the Chartered Company was involved. It was written by one Tanser and published in a book called *The Rhodesian Heritage*. The book is part of a series of what is called *The Rhodesiana*.

A Matabele warrior, after fulfilling all the military requirements under the Matabele Code which bound everyone not to marry until one had fulfilled its requirements, decided to get married. There was a virgin who had been waiting for him all these years, and after the warrior paid 30 head of cattle as a bride price, a day was set for the couple's marriage. It so happened that they had to register the marriage at the District Commissioner's office, and the DC heard about the wedding. He quickly invited the couple to a reception at his official residence. At the official residence of this seemingly wonderful official, the groom was then sent away – possibly at gunpoint –

without his bride to be. The story as narrated by Tanser is scarce on detail but does state that the bride emerged from the DC's residence sobbing the following morning. If Rhodes heard about it, we are not told. If he heard about it, what did he do? But why did Tanser have the incident published? Perhaps to warn the Chartered Company that they had responsibility that they could not treat the African as mere sex objects.

Let me close this sad chapter on Lobengula's children by returning briefly to the subject of the so-called Rhodes' correspondent. Ranger says the correspondent urged Rhodes to quietly get rid of Njube. I am convinced that Ranger knew the correspondent because there is a confidential file among Ranger's references.

Can the reader imagine what scandal would have resulted from his identification or naming the correspondent? Can the reader imagine the *Cape Argus* newspaper coming out with the following headline: "The Colossus Urged 'To Get Rid' of Lobengula's Son" or the opposition *Cape Times* with a poser 'Rhodes in A Fix over Lobengula?"

No, I just cannot see that happening because Ranger suffered cold feet! After all, he is not a journalist looking for a scoop but an historian (and a good one for that matter) but armed with that confidential file a reputable newspaper would have published and be damned. The welfare of Lobengula's children is a matter of profound public interest, and no newspaper worthy of the name would cover it up. This was a human-interest story of the year.

After all, had the Princes been allowed to develop their full potential only Rhodes or the Chartered Company had everything to gain from treating them - the survivors of the Company's arch-enemy - like fellow human beings. That they failed to do so shows the depth of xenophobia the Imperial Government and the Company harboured against the Matabele. The death of both Njube and Nguboyenja marked a punctuation in the Great Purge of the Matabele Monarchy which were in due course followed by Nyamande's death. It was this cruel purging of the Matabele Royal Family by those who used the right of conquest to destroy a kingdom.

CHAPTER 21

MUGABE DISOWNS GWEBU PEOPLE

IN February 2004, I was still a member of the Media and Information Commission.

It was during my stay in Harare to attend a monthly meeting of the MIC that I noticed the morning television news which was preceded by telling the country that "the Nguni threw Shona people into the Chinhoyi Cave Pool". This was a bit of fanatical piece of mythology dressed up as history. The broadcast apparently had been going on, unnoticed, for years, possibly since Independence. It was a blatant and shameful hate broadcast by the national broadcaster against the Nguni people, and I determined to do something about it.

The Chief Executive of the Zimbabwe Broadcasting Corporation, Rino Zhuwarara was also a member of the MIC and I approached him and demanded to know what in the name of sanity the ZBC was doing inciting a section of the population against another. I declared, "If you don't remove that stuff from the news bulletin, I will write to the President and complain". I was, of course, bluffing because I knew that the broadcast was not without President Mugabe's approval. But there was a danger that, if I went ahead and complained as I had threatened, this could be picked up by the private media and prove embarrassing to the government. The man, however, did not call my bluff.

I was fuming and the man looked at me for a long while as if he had seen a monster. After recovering from his shock, with an apology, he explained.

"You are right. But I can't just remove it. Give me time," he said in a conciliatory tone of voice. Six weeks later, the offending report was gone. I had walked from confronting this man to the office of the Executive Chairman of the Commission, Dr. Tafataona Mahoso to ask him how that news report was helping in nation-building. The man was dumbfounded. I had done something positive toward the cause of nation building, so I thought, but I was just fooling myself. Those were the days when I still believed that government needed time to make an honest and diligent effort towards the needful subject of nation-building. There was a need for some serious exercise to clean up the blood-splattered image of the government and a horrendous stinking egg in Mugabe's face. But I was deluding myself. After all the rallying song says, 'ZANU is a party of blood' and it has been taken up by the G40 who were not born when our glorious liberation struggle raged. But whose blood in peacetime Zimbabwe is the song calling for? Another unpleasant surprise awaited me.

It came two years later in February 2006, the season to celebrate President Robert Mugabe's birthday. This annual event drew people – mostly young people – from all over the country. On that year, it was being hosted by the Manicaland City of Mutare. He had been addressing the gathering when, for some reason, he raised the subject of the Gwebu community in Buhera. "Gwebu people in Buhera are not our people", he said.

In the gathering were people from Matabeleland who were there to pay their respects to the man but were obviously unwelcome. The Gwebu people originally came from Esigodini, south of Bulawayo, in the 1920s. They had been removed from their land to be settled in one of the most barren communal lands of the country, 300 km away. Esigodini is the African name for an area in Umzingwani District which became known as Essexvale, where

Frederick Courtney Selous had pegged out his 200 000-acre farm in line with the Victoria Secret Agreement of August 1893. In the same district, there were other settlers like Arthur Rhodes who "owned" 50 000 acres of land taken from the African people. So Chief Gwebu's people were moved to Buhera where they are still considered aliens.

Their removal from the land followed the recommendations of the Carter Land Commission. Ndebele people at Mugabe's birthday bash were there to pay their respects to the man and wish him many more. But the fact that he chose the occasion to disown them goes to show how deep his hatred of the Ndebele people is. Mugabe has an extremely vindictive and callous character. In my view, nothing demonstrates his disposition better than his treatment of Didymus Mutasa, a veteran of the liberation struggle. After the ZBC experience two years earlier, this became the last straw in my hope for a meaningful change of policy of sectarianism; the foundation upon which the government of Zimbabwe is hurtling at a break-neck speed towards the establishment of a totalitarian one-party state. Standing next to him as he made his remarks about the Gwebu community was Absalom Sikhosana, the national president of the Youth League of the ruling Zanu-PF from Matabeleland. Mugabe's Matabelephobia knows no bounds. How then can anyone say Mugabe has expressed regret that he set up a military unit to commit genocide in Matabeleland and the Midlands where the Ndebele people could be found?

The people of Matabeleland are often told to shut up about the *Gukurahundi* (it has been revised to become "Gukuradzviti" to emphasise the idea that the Ndebele people are the enemy) issue. It is said Mugabe apologised by calling it an act of madness. If he ever did that, not many people in Matabeleland are aware of it. Apologising would go against the grain of the man's callous and unforgiving character which is tinged with arrogant impunity. How could he apologise while at the same time making a law to protect himself and those who committed the crime?

Mugabe is still the same man who called on Tony Blair to rule his England "and let me rule my Zimbabwe". But Tony Blair is not guilty of sending a brigade to kill off innocent civilians in one half of his country. That is just one fundamental difference between Blair and Mugabe. The fact that Mugabe often receives standing ovations from his fellow travellers at the UN General Assembly is a matter for the record. These are leaders of African states whose right to be members of the UN is indeed questionable.

Their economies are reeling in the mud after years of being subjected to kleptomania and their ordinary citizens are wallowing in abject poverty. Zimbabwe is a leading member of Africa's zombie economies. These economies are neither dead no alive. But they have bloated armies while the country's' hospitals are operating without essential drugs and mortuaries are reeking with the smell of dead bodies

Robert Mugabe created what the Spanish people call an *imbroglio* – a complicated, difficult, unfathomable, unpleasant, dreadful and embarrassing situation. But he presided over that economy and enjoying every moment of it despite a political landscape that was splattered with the blood of innocent minority tribes in his country. And yet Zimbabwe was the only country in Africa that boasted a military university while there was no visible enemy or threat from anyone in the continent or out. So what was the reason for flirting with nuclear power North Korea when the only perceived threat from the Matabele Warriors was removed by Great Britain in 1893?

In 2013 Emmerson Mnangagwa was reported as telling an election rally in support of his wife in his home area, without batting an eyelid that he went abroad "to learn to kill". He was addressing his own people. This is dreadful to the people of Matabeleland and the Midlands. President Emmerson Mnangagwa while still a Vice President had, on two occasions, since 2011 led a strong delegation of government officers and party stalwarts to appear before the UN Universal Periodic Review in Geneva to defend the government's human rights record. A report of the UPR for 2016 says submissions by the Zimbabwe "could easily be refuted as clear misrepresentation of the actual situation on ground", according to one UPR report following the 2016 review. Zimbabwe and Uganda are the only two African countries where violations of human rights are still common.

A newsletter published by Zimbabwe Lawyers for Human Rights, *The Legal Monitor*, reports:

"Notably, CSOs from Zimbabwe presented to the UPR Advocacy Charter which noted among other issues the delay in implementing the provisions of the Constitution of Zimbabwe (Amendment 20 of 2013) concerns that the national human rights institution being ZHRC continue to be undermined by the executive, concerns over state actions that perpetuate violation of freedom of assembly and association, lack of protection for Human Rights Defenders, police brutality on citizenry while exercising their constitutional right to demonstrate coupled with a general state of impunity which still persists to date".

The report also features the whereabouts of missing journalist and human rights activist Itai Dzamara. Concerning claims by the Zimbabwe delegation in Geneva in 2016 that the Government was working with Dzamara's family to establish his whereabouts, and that these claims "could easily be refuted as clear misrepresentation of the actual situation on the ground". This was Robert Mugabe's Zimbabwe.

There can be no doubt he enjoyed every minute of ruling his own backyard with an iron fist. He was greatly flattered by fellow tyrants in the UN who never lost an opportunity to give him a standing ovation whenever he crossed swords with the likes of Tony Blair. The UN Charter provides protection to dictatorships under cover of what is called the rights of a sovereign state. The so-called sovereign nation can persecute its own citizens with impunity and still attend UN assemblies to be cheered by fellow travellers.

The 2013 Constitution of Zimbabwe has a limited provision for devolution of power to enable participation in government of the country at the local level. This legal instrument is being flagrantly subverted by the government with impunity. They do so by usurping the authority of local authorities in the function of employment of local people to participate in their own government, to give expression to the letter and spirit of devolution as provided for in the Constitution.

The Central Government, through the Ministry of Local Government, employs key personnel for local councils, district and provincial administration. The appointed officers, in turn, employ people from their own areas, with serious and devastating consequences for regions like occupied Matabeleland. The universal exclusion policies of first Robert Mugabe and now Emmerson Mnangagwa' government has pushed the victims of tribalism into the deep end of despair for 40 years.

But the Shona identity gets a little blurred and lost in the polyglot of the tribes who generally call themselves Mashona because a good number of them have only become Shona during the last 100 years or so when the name "Shona" gained currency. Until then, the name "Shona" did not exist as part of their language or culture. Their adoption of the name "Shona" became an unquestionable part of their culture since the advent of the white man. Its origin, therefore, begins with colonialism and has been strengthened with attainment of independence when the ruling Axis of Tribalism has become an unassailable military and political power. One can name any number of these ethnic groups who originally came from neighbouring nations and only found themselves in Mashonaland through migration.

To return to the subject of Shona mythology, it is said a spirit medium foresaw the advent of "kneeless people" (they wore pants that covered their knees down to their ankles) who would occupy the territory and later be driven away. The fact that the white man came with arms of war and was welcome for a while before being driven out 110 years later, makes the spirit medium's prediction credible, one would say. But there is something missing: This is the fact that, 52 years before the white man arrived Mzilikazi occupied Matabeleland and found no Mashona in effective presence there. There was furthermore no spirit medium to predict his arrival or the fact that his warriors wore skin aprons and carried assegais! But according to history books in use in the country Matabeleland (the territory was then known as Mthwakazi) the territory he settled in to build a kingdom was under the control of the Mashona! This is the kind of adulterated history that spawns fanaticism.

Shona historians are at great pains to deny that the Mashona involvement in the 1896 uprising was an accident of history which owes its reality to a man named Mukwati (Makwati), a Matabele warrior who first led the uprising in Matabeleland when it broke out. He fought in the Battle of Intaba ZikaMambo before going up north to start the uprising in Mashonaland. Being a Tonga captured in Monze by the Matabele warriors', Mukwati was neither Shona nor Ndebele. It will be seen, therefore, that mythology is not an accurate yardstick with which to determine one's identity. It is nothing but a pack of wishful thinking and a contrived make-believe nonsense!

This is a long and emotive subject but for now let me pose a question: how does the reader understand the fact that the land grab by the British government affected both sides, although there is nothing to show that the people of Mashonaland offered any protest against occupation of their own territory in the first place, and their failure to oppose recommendations of the Morris Carter Commission which closed the chapter on the land question for all time? Is it unthinkable that through the occupation of Mashonaland in 1890 the colonist, in a strategy to win the support of one of the two sides, deliberately played one against the other? The same cannot be said though about Mzilikazi whose policy was *Isizwe ka selukwe* (let the nation be knit together) from all the tribes, without exception, he met on the way to Matabeleland or those he found in the land between Limpopo and the Zambezi.

Before I return to the subject of the petition, let me observe that a question was raised as to the response of the people of Mashonaland and those of Matabeleland to the decision of the Privy Council of 1919 which rejected African claims on land that had been taken from them. On page 67 of Professor Terence Ranger's book, *The African Voice in Southern Rhodesia (1970)* the following is how he answers it:

There was in fact little articulate response in Mashonaland, though the affected tribesmen who had to move out of the areas ceded to European occupation remembered it with bitterness for many years. But in Matabeleland a movement of protest on a wide scale began to develop. It was still the Ndebele who had the greatest grievance over land'.

These sentiments are also expressed by the Superintendent of Natives following the Carter Commission of 1914.

The Matabele people had already died in their tens of thousands trying to stop invasion by a foreign power using superior arms of war. But it is noteworthy that the affected tribesmen in Mashonaland merely remembered their deprivation with mere bitterness for many years! But then who has given them *legitimacy* to rule over Matabeleland with an iron rod? It is the British people through the skulduggery of the Chartered Company and the Imperial Government.

CHAPTER 22

THE RIGHT OF CONQUEST INSANITY

DURING the heydays of colonialism and imperialism, there was an agreement or understanding known as "The Right of Conquest". Under this unwritten agreement, boundaries were drawn up and became sacrosanct.

This tradition allowed the conquering powers to subject the conquered people to murderous massacres or extermination of whole native tribes without being called to account. There was no such thing as war crimes. The conquering powers could commit crimes against humanity without fear of being called to book. In short, the victims of imperialism and colonialism were often treated like animals of the wild. They could be shot for entertainment or abused in the most flagrant and barbaric manner without repercussions. The law of the jungle among the colonists and imperialists had for years a free run without a prick of conscience.

For example, there were hundreds of Africans from South Africa, the Khoi Sans who were taken to Europe to become inmates of 'human zoos' where they were paraded for public entertainment and amusement.

This entertainment also often turned the victims into sex objects for which the public paid up front, to satisfy their perverted sexual appetites. The result was that hundreds of the victims died miserable deaths from venereal diseases. This is just one example of inhuman and horrific treatment of victims of the right of conquest.

However, the tradition of the right of conquest gradually changed after World II and "The War of

Aggression" was proscribed under the so-called Nuremberg Principles. This was followed in 1974 by the United Nations resolution 3314 which frowns on aggression without making it unlawful. It is, therefore, notable that despite the sovereign rights of a state, aggression has not become a thing of the past and is unlikely to become so in the foreseeable future. The merits and demerits of aggression are many and varied and the debate about them can become highly polemic.

For instance, it can be argued that aggression should be sanctioned where international peace is under threat and human life exposed to danger. In such cases, there is an added danger that the aggressing powers will demand regime change. We have a classic example of the bloody shambles in Haiti in 2004 when an international peace-keeping force led by the United States led to the death of more innocent citizens than had been witnessed under the ousted regime of Aristead.

But there is no denying the fact that indeed regime change, depending on a variety of reasons and motives, may become necessary but the polemics of such a move have nothing to do with international law. Such moves have been shown to be a game in a self-justification strategy of the powerful. But there is an added danger that any given situation can be manipulated to justify regime change, leading to the violation of the tenets of democracy.

One can name any number of examples where aggression was necessary to save lives. This can be done without the aggressor seeking permanent occupation of the aggressed state. A case in point is the former Yugoslavia where NATO forces went in to rescue beleaguered nations that were being subjected to horrific bloodshed.

In eastern Democratic Republic of Congo, the UN has been there for years to keep a fragile peace from total collapse.

Aggression under certain circumstances, therefore,

can be justified and become a defensible feature of international law for a term, even if such aggression is not authorized by a UN resolution. But there are glaring inconsistencies and ambiguities in the application of the principle. For instance, the Butcher of Spain, General Franco was allowed a 40-year run without anyone stepping in to stop him, even though the Spanish civil war began ten years before the end of World War II and was still raging long after the end of the war and the onset of the Nuremberg Rules. Franco's reign of terror only came to an end in 1974 when the General met his Waterloo in death.

During nearly 40 years of his rule, Franco executed 150 000, sent 500 000 more to prison and another one million fled the country. There was no intervention by parties in the Nuremberg arrangement. In neighbouring Portugal, Salazar and his neighbour in Greece also had opened galleries of murder with European superpowers as spectators.

Many people still do not know whether or not Saddam Hussein and Muamar Gaddafi had amassed weapons of mass destruction to warrant aggressive occupation and destruction of their countries. But it is noteworthy that before his turn came after the invasion of Kuwait, Saddam Hussein had been sponsored and equipped to invade Iran.

There can be no argument, therefore, that Saddam Hussein was not a saint and was known to rush in where angels fear to tread. Saddam Hussein had a private army known as MKO which had been created to invade Iran and Kuwait and threaten other neighbours. Even so, was it proper to murder them rather than bringing them before an appropriate international court of law? The rule of law should not be compromised by the application of martial law, especially where self-justification appears to have influenced the decision to invade Iraq and Libya.

There is a tragic contradiction in all this because in Liberia, Serbia and Ivory Coast conflicts, for instance, culprits in the flow of innocent blood that was witnessed in these countries were treated civilly to face justice at the international level. The influence of parties to the Nuremberg Trials was visible in these three cases.

So, it can be argued that Gaddafi and Hussein should not have been executed without trial in an open international court of justice. It can further be argued that the use of martial law to deal with them was, therefore, inappropriate.

Their execution, as a result became an act of self-justification by the powers that destroyed Iraq and Libya. Self-justification has become an instrument of wrongdoing in international conflicts where aggression, wrongly or not, became necessary.

There is a need, consequently, to avoid the danger of compromising the essence of the rule of law and the dispensation of justice in international affairs. It is imperative that any needful aggression should be sanctioned by a UN resolution. This is the only way through which the rule of law, always used by the aggressor for selfish ends to justify an unlawful act, can be protected to avoid the sham to which this ideal is often reduced by unlawful self-justification.

In my country, Mthwakazi, known today as Matabeleland, a tragic miscarriage of justice was witnessed in 1889. Paramount Chief Lotshe Hlabangana was executed for allegedly misleading King Lobengula over the notorious Rudd Concession.

Two white missionaries testified that the Concession authorized the Chartered Company to mine gold wherever the precious metal could be found including the King's Palace!

The truth of the matter is that the Concession did not grant the Company such rights. The Rudd Concession did not even grant the Chartered Company the right to effectively occupy any part of Matabeleland or Mashonaland. But this gross and tragic misinterpretation of the Concession cost Lotshe and his extended family their lives. However, Lotshe admitted his role in the drafting of the document for the King's signature and was convicted. The execution of his extended family, however, was a massacre for which the King could, under the Nuremberg Rules, have been dragged before a court of law to be tried for mass murder. His extended family had nothing to do with the Rudd Concession.

The execution of Saddam Hussein and Muamar Kaddafi, therefore, provides a questionable parallel under the rules of the Nuremberg Principles, which rules did not authorize that the accused be put before a wall to be shot.

The accused were tried - albeit in a military setting - and this presupposes that they had a right to defend themselves. The trouble is that Libya and Iraq were victims of self- justification by superpowers that invaded the two countries.

But when an accused is denied legal representation, miscarriage of justice becomes the end result. It is like abducting and subjecting a victim to enforced disappearance.

Justice and the rule of law should not be compromised in this manner by champions of democracy. There is an interesting case involving Zimbabwe where the Government, in another glaring self-justification and bloody enterprise launched genocide against a minority of its citizens in the 1980s. It is my argument that the principals who ordered the operation but cannot be arrested to be brought before an international court of justice, can lawfully be tried in absentia before a court of justice at the international level although they will be free to appoint legal representatives to defend them. The death of innocent civilians in a staged "dissident" uprising in Zimbabwe must be mitigated even though those who committed the crimes have defied calls for reparations. In the dispensation of justice, the accused should not escape punishment by default by using the UN Charter.

Let us return to the subject of the right of conquest during the heyday of imperialism and colonialism and see what happened.

It is not my intention to suggest that the kind of barbarism that was applied against the conquered during the scramble for Africa was limited to the treatment of Africans in this manner. There is no shortage of evidence that Europeans who opposed the establishment in a conflict situation in Europe during the Reformation, for instance, were treated similarly.

I must cite the cases of Stalinist Russia and Nazi Germany because what happened in their cases was the norm under the right of conquest rules. One must read the history of the Soviet Story for a shocking insight into the cruelty and barbarism against the victims of the system. Stalin was, however, not a monopolist in such horrors under the right of conquest and the perpetration of its insanity. However, Western European governments or nations have been known to distance themselves from such horrors by conveniently eclipsing their own fair share in such horrors.

The Spanish Civil War, among other shameful by-products of self-justification in Europe, was allowed to continue for nearly 40 years without intervention by the so-called Superpowers who became disinterested spectators as Franco indulged his thirst for innocent blood.

In the United Kingdom, those who disagreed with the Church of England, like Crammer, Tyndale and Rogers died horrifying deaths at the stake. During the Dark Ages, for another example, victims of religious persecution were also put to the stake to be burnt alive. Scores of millions died under these conditions. The Papacy under Pope Benedict has admitted culpability and apologized. But those who colonised Africa and other areas of the world have not felt the remorse to apologise for excesses they committed in their treatment of Africans, and their bloody expeditions have remained tinged with the sin racism.

During the French Revolution of 1798, for yet another example, Napoleon Bonaparte's forces committed heinous crimes against fellow Frenchmen, women and children. The details are many and well known and need no repetition. Nothing will be gained by dwelling upon them.

France was literally bleeding, as a single bloody episode in its history rudely pushed France away from the worship of God, to paganism and the worship of a goddess of reason. Atheism became the religion of the country.

Those of France's captains of industry, its merchants, its bankers, its scholars, artists, inventors, farmers, doctors of medicine and religious leaders, who managed to escape the carnage, fled the country in droves to areas of the world where they could find refuge or establish colonies. And their flight set France back perhaps 100 years.

By how many years did the invasion of Iraq and Libya by rogue superpowers set the two countries back? Why are Europe and its western allies silent about what is happening in Yemen and Palestine?

Why is Europe ashamed to admit that the flood of African and Arab refugees into Europe is a result of self-justification by western allies who destroyed Libya and are now helping to destroy Syria and are threatening other states in the Middle East?

What perhaps is sad about France's experience during the Revolution is the fact that, 320 years after the event, it is still celebrated in the country on Bastille Day. The French celebrate the wiping out of a wedding party and the massacre of 50 000 innocent souls in one mad night.

But can the well-known records of atrocities against fellow citizens, who happen to hold a different view or belief, be equated to anything that Mzilikazi or Lobengula committed against anyone, European or African during the heyday of the right of conquest?

Although the rules of the right of conquest meant that the imperialists and colonists did not care what happened to their victims, the practice appears to have declined somewhat in the 1970s, without disappearing altogether. Moreover, the formation of the United Nations after World War II, which proffered hope for humanity, has not prevented aggression during which heinous crimes against populations of the affected nations become commonplace.

It is, therefore, to be regretted that the UN is being subverted and rendered impotent by the very champions of its foundation, leaving the world without an alternative to champion the causes of decency, morality, the rule of law, justice and democracy. There is no acceptable alternative to democracy and the rule of law. The world can never have enough of the above-named fundamental ideals in a universe in which evil self-justification has taken centre stage to cause turmoil.

Since the formation of the UN, the world has been lurched to the brink of the so-called New World Order, which in turn promises to become a New World Disorder. And the rogue superpowers are visible in the causes of turmoil that grips many parts of the world today.

Can this threatening calamitous disorder be forestalled or fixed? The answer is an emphatic "No!" The disorder is already on-going. This phenomenon is despite the constraining force of the UN Charter. A wilful superpower can ignore the provisions of the UN Charter with impunity. And in many cases the UN Charter is used by governments to defend unlawful acts in their domains or abroad to protect self-interest. The main offenders against democracy today are not to be found in Africa, Asia or the Middle East but from the self-justifying superpowers in the west. In asserting this view, I am not acquitting African and Asian countries of any wrongdoing.

Far from declaring these regions guiltless in this regard, I am simply recognizing the morality that those who make the rules must be the first to obey them. Proponents of democracy in the west are not obeying their own rules for democracy to become a universally accepted ideal. They must lead by example and avoid double standards. This failure on their part has plunged the world into a chasm of conflict in which the world is stuck today.

But what happened to nations like the Matabele Kingdom during the run of The Right of Conquest in the 19th century cannot be ignored or simply treated with cynical flippancy because the crimes that were committed against the people were carried out under the banner of the white man's civilization.

Can crimes against humanity and civilization ever become bedfellows by blatantly crossing the red line between good and evil?

There was once a time when the oppressed people of the world looked to the First World, in which the evolution of democratic principles had long taken root, for protection. This privilege is no more.

In Africa for instance, the call was loud and clear (and still is) for African governments to accept and entrench the principles of democracy as a way of life. During the past 60 years of Africa's independence, however, many African states have drifted away from the democracy clarion call to embrace totalitarianism and autocracy where the ruled are subjected to the vagaries of tribalism and one-party rule.

The quality of life among ordinary Africans has sharply declined to levels far below the level at which colonial rulers left it. This is evidenced by the tens of thousands of Africans who are dying trying to cross the waves of death into Europe where they hope to find better life.

Their rights to protest this sharp decline in the quality of their living standards are being bludgeoned by the rules of one-party rule and the vicious propaganda by the rulers to coerce the ruled to toe the line. Democracy in Africa has no sporting chance to win. Most of the ruled in states in which one-party rule is the order of the day tragically live in a state of perpetual fear to protest. In Zimbabwe, for one example, those who have protested misgovernment have disappeared without trace.

These conditions of poverty are evidenced by the sharp rise in street vending in most African countries. This situation is being exploited by African governments which use donor food for their political gain by claiming credit for the alleviation of hunger. The "orphans" of colonialism like the people of Matabeleland and the Midlands in Zimbabwe, have been left out in the cold of a one-party dictatorship.

Many African states today see the principles of democracy as neo-colonialism to be fought. In my own country, for instance, the philosophy of African Democracy, the principle of majority rule, has been embraced and is used to oppress and persecute minority groups who believe in the philosophy of African Nationalism. The principle of Majority Rule is, therefore, repugnant because it precludes minority groups from the good of belonging and turns them into "dissidents" to be hunted down. They are denied these rights by the application of discrimination which is akin to what happened in apartheid ruled South Africa.

It is a system that gives licence to the majority tribe to oppress and persecute minority tribes with impunity, with the blanket application of the policy of cruel exclusivity. This policy denies minority groups social, educational and economic benefits to which every citizen is entitled. All this is due to the fact that tribalism has a greater appeal to the rulers, than democracy and the need to build a truly united nation in a diverse ethnic environment.

The surge towards totalitarianism and the

entrenchment of one-party rule in Africa is spiralling out of control, and African governments are drifting away from such international conventions as the International Criminal Court of Justice, unconstrained by the UN Charter.

African governments often quote their rights under the UN Charter as defence for their ill-treatment of their own people.

There is, moreover, a visible conflict of interest between the extent to which the UN Charter can be invoked to protect the sovereignty of a state and its territorial integrity, on the one hand, and the protection of human rights within the same state, on the other. More often than not, the interest of human life and other rights lose the contest to the interest of the state because those in power are not squeamish about shedding the blood of their own citizens and the UN can do nothing about it.

The supposed pervasive powers of the UN Charter, however, have not stopped squealing by African Governments about their being alleged innocent victims of criticism when they treat their own people in this manner! They often cry foul by alleging that former colonial rulers were hell-bent on what is called neo-colonialism.

Does this mean that African states have not learnt anything of value in governance during the 60 years of self-rule? In contrast, their ability to remain in power by hook or crook for decades during which misrule of citizens is the order of the day, is well-known.

African governments are generally intolerant of dissent or opposition and will not refrain from using violence to destroy opposition.

During the 2011 Ivory Coast, conflict something diplomatically complicated, difficult to understand and must have been extremely embarrassing to the African Union, happened. The imbroglio remains a mystery.

French troops stormed the underground Chamber where Laurent Gbagbo and his wife were hiding and refusing to surrender power after losing an election. And, thanks to the intervention by France, the couple were carried out of the country to face justice. In the streets of the capital Abidjan, South African Marines were patrolling, watched by United Nations observers. Their presence in Abidjan remains a mystery.

For months, the people of Ivory Coast had been killing each other amid reports that an Eminent Person was trying to negotiate a cessation of hostilities between the reluctant Head of State in the South and his in-coming opposite number in the north. He was not making much headway amid rumours that the out-going Gbagbo was sticking to his guns, arguing that he was protected under the UN Charter. This provision of the Charter is called the sovereignty and territorial integrity of a state. Many countries use the UN Charter to commit crimes against humanity, even those who are citizens. But he had lost an election.

France, ignoring his protestations, simply ordered its troops in and flushed him out of his hideout and the civil war came to an end. France was not authorised by a UN resolution.

Joseph Taylor of Liberia, after his arrest, was reported as regretting that he had not listened to Robert Mugabe's advice for him to stay put, using the UN Charter as a shield. When French troops raided the hideout where Gbagbo was hiding, the SA Marines were not ordered to engage French troops, and this averted a bloody standoff between the two sides. This lesson was apparently ignored in the Central African Republic where in 2013 South African troops were involved in a bloody clash with rebels and lost a number of men.

A question that must be asked is: Were the French

troops and the South African Marines on the same side and whose side was it?

The punchline of the Ivory Coast episode is not so much the fact that France's intervention brought the bloody civil war to an eventual end. It is the fact that the South African Marines were there at all. There is nothing to show they represented anyone. I am not, for a moment, suggesting that France intervened purely in the interest of the people of Ivory Coast. The country is a former French colony and France has other interests in its former colony.

It is my argument, however, that the intervention saved thousands of lives of the people of this great country. It is said Ivory Coast has since become one of Africa's fastest growing economies today.

France's intervention in another African conflict in Mali in 2013 has brought relative peace to that country. It is noteworthy that France's intervention in Mali was, believably, also not sanctioned by the UN.

Another punchline of the Ivory Coast episode, and the one factor that boggles the mind, is the fact that the SA Marines were not there under the auspices of the United Nations or the AU. The vexing question that remains unanswered in this regard relates to the source of authority for the Marine's presence in Abidjan. Did the South African Parliament authorize the deployment of the Marines in Ivory Coast?

According to UN sources, former South African President Thabo Mbeki was in Abidjan talking to Laurent Gbagbo at the time. Can he be associated with the deployment of the marines in anyway and can this association be extended to the government in South Africa? To hazard an answer to this question, one must first accept that the marines were not mercenaries looking for someone to hire them for a hazardous mission.

These men and women were regulars, professionals in national garb. The only conclusion that one must draw from these facts, therefore, is that they represented the government of South Africa. But that will not wash. They could not be there outside of the auspices of the UN but as representing the Republic.

The UN and the Republic were supposed to be working together to bring peace to the civil war-torn country. There is, moreover, nothing to show that the marines represented the AU either.

Many questions were left hanging.

One of them is: Was the presence of the Marines a result of some "silent diplomacy" of sorts? Would such a development involve Jacob Zuma's government? This is unthinkable. South Africa is a constitutional democracy. Would the government require the approval of Parliament, as it is believed this was the case in 2013 in the case of the Central African Republic? If so, why did the Marines cause such a stir and raised eyebrows among UN observers in Abidjan? What was the role of the AU in all this?

After all it is an open secret that the AU has no money to burn. Look at its shameful failure for several months to bankroll peace-keeping operations in South Sudan. Another burning question concerns the United States in Somalia where American drones are slaughtering innocent civilians? It appears there is a third force working with terrorists in Somalia. On the other hand the money-strapped AU is reported to have taken delivery of a "gift hall" from China in recent years, to facilitate the dumping of that endless range of Chinese kitsch to bolster growth of Africa's exploding street vending industry, while African textile mills, left behind by the departing colonial rulers, have remained mothballed for the better part of 60 years!

It is further reported that the AU is waiting to take delivery of a facility to house its Peace and Security

Commission from a member of the European Union? Can the AU still claim it is a non-aligned bulwark between the West and the East?

Another question is: Who pays those who are assigned to mediate in conflict situations in Africa? Is it the host government, the UN or the African Union? Couldn't it better if the task was left to the UN? After all, African members of the world body, like all others, pay subscriptions for their right to expect the UN to mediate in conflict situations on the continent. It then would be left to the UN to invite members to send units of their army to assist in peace keeping operations.

Mediation by Eminent Persons in Africa has a dark record of failure, and this record has been worsened by Africa's inability to pay for peace keeping operations on the continent. Moreover, mediation by the so-called Eminent Persons is wide open for abuse. What is to stop the affected government and the mediator coming (for a fee, of course) to some arrangement to frustrate mediation efforts? Does the failure in Darfur owe its fate to this fundamental weakness in mediation by Eminent Persons in Africa?

As a Zimbabwean I can never forget that one of Africa's Eminent Persons, Thabo Mbeki, displayed unpardonable partiality when he openly rebuked Morgan Tsvangirai for alleged disrespect towards Robert Mugabe. His much-vaunted 'silent diplomacy' suffered a serious dent as a result, while Robert Mugabe often went scot-free when he threatened to give Tsvangirai a bloody nose for refusing to submit to the dictator. Tsvangirai was moved to declare that Mbeki was not fit to be mediator in Africa, and many would agree with him.

There was a lot of speculation in Zimbabwe that Mbeki was in Robert Mugabe's payroll. In the Ivorian capital during the presence of the SA Marines in the country, there were unconfirmed reports that the former South African head of state landed in Abidjan in a private jet. There are so many thorny issues about these missions.

Is the pension of a former Head of State – even in prosperous South Africa – enough to buy or hire a private jet to enable a mediator to visit a country in conflict?

There are so many thorny and imponderable issues about these missions. To whom are those involved in mediation accountable? Are they paid for results or their time? And can anyone say the payer gets value for money for these bloody transactions.

During an African Union fund-raising conference in November 2018 during which it was announced that the grouping had raised millions of dollars for its peace-keeping operations, former South African President Thabo Mbeki said in the past the AU could not raise a paltry $50 000 to finance peace-keeping operations in Africa. This is a fact.

But was it for Mbeki to make such a brazen statement about the cost of negotiating peace in Africa when his record as an Eminent Person in this field is so dismal? Can Africa afford to pay this amount for failure? Is it really cheap for the AU to pay this amount instead of raising a peace-keeping force like Uganda and Kenya have done in Somalia? In 1998, Zimbabwe sent a unit of its army to the Democratic Republic of Congo to prop up Kabila's regime.

This caused a lot of nasty comment and questions among economists and other observers in the country. It was reported that, while they were there, the army unit seized opportunities to get involved in commercial enterprises with units of the DRC army. This was noticed by some observers.

The Minister of Defence at the time, Moven Mahachi was forced to admit that the Zimbabwean mission in the DRC had been involved in "income-generating projects" to finance the mission because Zimbabwe was short of money. It was a national scandal.

But national scandals do not make any difference in Zimbabwe because there is no shortage of those who are often scapegoated, like Tony Blair, for the failed and corrupt state that has become Zimbabwe. The government is not accountable to anyone but itself.

South Africa under Jacob Zuma has announced its intention to join a number of African states that have announced their withdrawal from the International Criminal Court of Justice. ICCJ is a voluntary body which seeks to promote transparency in governance.

Is this an indication that the African National Congress government is toying with an idea of tampering with the constitution to keep the ANC in power? If so, nothing would legitimize the racist AWB (Afrikaner Resistance Movement) more than such a move.

In a country where the evils of racism have barely disappeared from the surface of every-day life, as nationals are still called by their racial distinctions by government leaders 22 years after the advent of democracy, a flashpoint of racial tensions is visibly lurking in the background. It will take interference with the constitution to reach a tipping point of racial conflict in South Africa.

If such interference became a fact, the ANC would lose its legitimacy as a democratic institution. The greatest losers in such an eventuality would be the African majority in the Republic and, of course, those of us in Zimbabwe where a black apartheid regime is in power. There are a number of reasons why this fear must be taken seriously. If the ANC adversely tampered with the constitution, white liberals in the fold of the DA can be expected to join forces with AWB, and such a development would fuel racial tensions and reverse the gains of democracy to the level of restoring apartheid in one form or the other. Healthy race relations must be cultivated in South Africa to avoid polarization among races in the Republic.

The ANC must avoid those temptations that might

lead to the inflammation of racial tensions in South Africa. It must avoid a situation that will give the AWB legitimacy. On the question of those who would suffer most in such an event, the most important truth is that, while the ANC still controls proceedings in parliament, the country's economy remains under the control of the white minority and a tipping point is unlikely to come soon enough to shift control to the black majority.

There is more over the armed forces factor. Has this changed to give black South Africans command? There is also the vexing question of land distribution.

The ANC government must resist the call to nationalise land Zimbabwean-style by politicians like Julius Malema. There is a heavy cost, in a variety of forms in areas of public life, attached to nationalisation of land and the government must use democratic means to find land for agriculture for aspiring black farmers and land for public works like housing.

Any amendment of the Constitution to facilitate acquisition of land must not interfere with democratic fundamentals. The constitution does not prevent government from acquiring land for essential national development. But wholesale nationalisation can precipitate unpredictable racial tensions and threaten national security. The emergence of organisations like the AWB in South Africa must have a place in democratic South Africa as long as such movements do not threaten security of the Republic.

Their existence is evidence that democracy is working in South Africa. White liberals in the country are unlikely to join movements like the AWB because this would be a huge throw-back to apartheid. Whites would not risk losing the admiration and support of friends they have made internationally since the end of apartheid. This, however, will depend on whether the ANC keeps its side of the bargain by abstaining from adversely interfering with the provisions of the democratic constitution. Such change would, say, take the form of extending the tenure of office beyond the present eight-year term, for one example.

South Africans should not be denied the right to remove a leader who threatens the tenets of democracy which are enshrined in the constitution. This applies to the leadership of the ANC as well.

The ANC must be prepared to accept change of government in South Africa because there is no acceptable alternative to democracy. The evils of the so-called African Democracy, such as is found in Zimbabwe, must be avoided in South Africa. African Democracy, as already said, is repugnant because it is oppressive and allows tyranny to thrive.

The Sons of Lobengula
(L-R) Nguboyenja, Njube and Sidojiwa

The Matabele King
Lobengula Khumalo
Reign September 1868 – January 1894

Cecil John Rhodes
Founder and Managing Director of British South Africa Company (BSAC)

Leander Starr Jameson
Administrator for Mashonaland in 1891. At the conclusion of the Matabele war 1893, Matabeleland was incorporated under Jameson's authority.

Maxim "Pom-Pom" Gun
The original version was capable of firing 600 one-pound shells per minute, and the psychological effect of its sound was awe-inspiring.

Chief Khayisa Ndiweni
Advocate of a federal State for Zimbabwe

Lancaster House Agreement

(R-L) Mr. R G Mugabe and Mr. J M Nkomo for the Patriotic Front, Sir I Gilmour and Lord Carrington – Chairman for the United Kingdom of Britain, Bishop A T Muzorewa and Dr. S C Mundawarara for Zimbabwe - Rhodesia

ABOUT AUTHOR

JONATHAN MAPHENDUKA

Jonathan Maphenduka is a retired Journalist who worked in Kenya and Zambia before joining *The Chronicle* in Bulawayo in 1965, retiring in 1998. His first book *The Rule by Conquest the Struggle in Mthwakazi* was published in 2015 and had a good run despite the fact that distribution was by cloak and dagger methods because the government frowned on the book due to its proposal for the establishment of Mthwakazi State embracing Matabeleland. He establishes in this book the fact that the hand of the British is visible in two genocides against the Matabele in the last century.

ABREVIATIONS AND ACRONYMS

ANC	African National Congress
AU	African Union
BSAC	British South Africa Company
ICC	International Criminal Court
Jameson Line	An official border between Zimbabwe and Mthwakazi, as signed in June 1891
MDC	Movement for Democratic Change
Mthwakazi	Mthwakazi is the traditional name of the proto-Ndebele and Ndebele kingdom that existed until the end of the 19th century within the area of today's Zimbabwe. Mthwakazi is widely used to refer to inhabitants of Matabeleland and Midlands provinces in Zimbabwe
PF	Patriotic Front
SADC	Southern African Development Community
UANC	The United African National Council
UDI	Unilateral Declaration of Independence
UK	United Kingdom

Umhlahlo Wesizwe Sika Mthwakazi	An umbrella cultural organisation that is dedicated to the restoration of the Mthwakazi state
UN	United Nations
UNFP	United National Federal Party
UPR	Universal Periodic Review
USD	United States of America Dollar
ZANU	Zimbabwe African National Union
ZANLA	Zimbabwe African National Liberation Army
ZAPU	Zimbabwe African People's Union
ZESA	Zimbabwe Electricity Supply Authority
ZIPRA	Zimbabwe People's Revolutionary Army
ZUPO	Zimbabwe United People's Organisation

BIBLIOGRAPHY

Baxter, Peter. *Rhodesia, Last Outpost of the British Empire 1890-1980.* Johannesburg. Galago Pub, 2010

Cobbing, Julian Raymond Dennis, *The Ndebele Under the Khumalos, 1820-1896.* Lancaster. University of Lancaster, 1976

Harris, John H. *The Chartered Millions.* London. Swarthmore Press, 1920

Ranger, Terence O. *The African Voice in Southern Rhodesia.* Evanston, IL. Northwestern University Press, 1970

Samkange, Stanlake. Origins of Rhodesia. New York. Frederick A Praeger, 1969

Selous, Frederick Courtney. *Sunshine and Storm in Rhodesia.* London. Rowland Ward & Co, 1896

Willis, W A and Collingridge LT. *The Downfall of Lobengula.* NewYork. Negro Universities Press, 1969

Credits

Any people depicted in stock imagery provided by Dollar Images are models, and such images are being used for illustrative purposes only.
Certain stock imagery © Dollar Stock Images

Cover Art "The 3 Princes" by Thamsanqa Khumalo

Proofreading Services by Felicity Mange

G

www.ingramcontent.com/pod-product-compliance
Lightning Source LLC
Chambersburg PA
CBHW071336080526
44587CB00017B/2854